ST. HELENA LIFELINE

RONNIE ERIKSEN

MALLETT & BELL PUBLICATIONS
THE CABINET
HIGH STREET
COLTISHALL
NORFOLK
NR12 7AA

Also by Ronnie Eriksen

The Sea was Kind to me (Amorique, Knysna 1990)

ISBN 0-620-15055-6

Dedicated
to my dear wife
Carol Diana Eriksen

ISBN 0-950-94353-3-1

© 1994 Ronnie Eriksen

Computer typeset by Rosemary Klein
and printed by Page Bros, Norwich
Bound by Western Book Company
Ltd, Bridgend, Mid Glamorgan.

CONTENTS

INTRODUCTION

It has given me a great deal of pleasure to have had the opportunity to write this account of courage, enterprise and initiative. The maritime history of South Africa, and the Cape trade in particular, is fascinating, and in taking up the challenge to provide a regular freight and passenger service to the islands of the South Atlantic and the Cape, Andrew Bell and the Curnow Shipping Company have added a further chapter to the saga of the southern seas.

To those who were regular travellers in the wide choice of passenger liners available up to the late 1960s, their gradual disappearance until none remained on the Cape run by the end of 1977, was nothing short of disaster.

One might well ask why, as late as 1963, Union-Castle Line should have entered into a new mail contract calling for an $11\frac{1}{2}$ day passage to the Cape?

For those in a hurry the airlines provided the wherewithal. Therefore, in the interest of operating economy, surely the answer should have been to opt for a 15 or even 16 day voyage, with sailings every fortnight? It is difficult to believe that the two passenger liners "Windsor Castle" and the "S.A.Vaal" could not have attracted sufficient patronage for those content to regard a leisurely relaxed ocean voyage as part of their holiday. When the time came to replace them, surely naval architects could have designed vessels equipped to carry containerised freight, with accommodation for 150 passengers at an economical speed of 16 knots.

It has been my privilege to have sailed in the ships of many Lines recorded in this narrative, from the "Kenilworth Castle" as a babe-in-arms in 1922 to the "Windsor Castle" on her last voyage down coast in 1977; and their departure brought to a close a period of gracious living I never expected to see again.

But the advent of the first RMS "St.Helena" on the Cape run in 1978 provided South Africans with the opportunity of once again travelling to the United Kingdom by sea. The success of this small ship, with her limited accommodation and passenger facilities, paved the way for the new "St.Helena", which sailed from Cardiff on her maiden voyage to Ascension, St. Helena and the Cape in November 1990.

Twice the size of her predecessor, the new RMS provide a standard of accommodation and passenger amenities which have revived that unique way of life only an ocean voyage can offer, and which I had feared was lost forever.

I am greatly indebted to Andrew Bell, his colleague Simon Sugrue, and the office staff of Curnow Shipping Ltd., for allowing me free access to their files and records, and for providing me with all the detailed information I required to prepare this book. Without their willing co-operation it could not have been written.

At this juncture I would like to make it perfectly clear that the views and opinions expressed in this narrative are entirely my own, and do not represent those of either the shipping companies or the individuals named in this book.

Ronnie Eriksen
Hove, Sussex, England
Knysna, E.Cape, South Africa
1990–1992.

ACKNOWLEDGEMENTS

I am grateful to Mr. Alan Mallett, author of "The Union Castle Line" and two other publications, for allowing me to include those photographs which appear in this book from his personal collection, and am further indebted to him for introducing me to Mr. Alex Duncan; Mr. Cliff Parsons of the World Ship Society; Mr. John Morgendaal of the Ship Society of South Africa, and through Mr. Morgendaal Mr. Robert Pabst; as well as the Hon, Mrs. ND Fischer Hoch.

The Hon Mrs. ND Fischer Hoch has graciously granted me permission to feature the print of her late father, Lord Kylsant; while the Ship Society of South Africa have been generous enough to make available to me photographs of the liners "Patria", " Principe Perfeito", "Europa", "Umtata", "Watussi", "Randfontein" and ""Duilio"". All were photographed by Mr. Robert Pabst, and the photograph of the "Duilio" is the property of Dr. E. Cornish, who has very kindly permitted its publication. The Society has moreover granted me permission to include the print of the liner "Ulysses" from Mr. Alan Mallett's collection.

I am also obliged to Mr. Alex Duncan, and to the World Ship Society, for permission to reproduce those photographs from Mr. Mallett's collection, for which they hold the copyright, and to Mr. Peter Kohler of Washington D C for permission to use photographs owned by him.

The remaining photographs are the property of Curnow Shipping Ltd and the St. Helena Shipping Co., and I am obliged to Mr. Andrew Bell for allowing me to publish them.

Finally I am deeply indebted to my Secretary, Mrs Joy Tennant for producing in South Africa the original typed manuscript for my publishers Mallett and Bell, whose advice has been invaluable, whose patience has been inexhaustible, and with whom it has been a pleasure to have been associated; as well as to Mrs. Janet Ansell in England for typing the revisions and amendments to the original manuscript prior to publication.

Ronnie Eriksen

I THE BEGINNING AND THE DEVELOPMENT OF THE CAPE PASSENGER TRADE: 1857–1900

Although it is recorded that in pre-Christian times the Phoenicians circumnavigated the African continent, many centuries were to elapse before South Africa, and the Cape itself, were rediscovered by the Portuguese navigator Bartholomew Diaz de Novaes in 1487, when seeking the sea route to India. Sailing down the west coast of Africa, Diaz had reached the mouth of the Orange River when a northerly gale drove his small craft southwards, well out of sight of the African coastline,

For almost a fortnight the gale persisted, and when calmer weather prevailed Diaz steered a northerly course until he made his landfall at what is known today as Mossel Bay, having unwittingly rounded the Cape in the process. Forced by his ship's company to abandon further search for a route to India, Diaz steered a westerly course before rounding the Cape on his return voyage to Portugal.

After his stormy passage south, Diaz named the Cabo Tormentos— Cape of Storms—later to be changed to Cape of Good Hope by King John II of Portugal, as its discovery opened up the sea route to India and all its riches.

Ten years later Vasco da Gama was sent to capitalise on Diaz's discovery, and after rounding the Cape and following the eastern shore line he reached what he named Natal, having made his discovery on Christmas Day 1497. Continuing on a north-easterly course da Gama discovered first Mombasa and Malindi before, no doubt following the advice of experienced Arab seamen, going onto reach the prized subcontinent at a place he named Goa.

The sea route to the East had been discovered, and English, French and Spanish vessels benefited from the courage and determination of the Portuguese mariners. In the 16th Century the East India Company was formed in London, and a regular service to India was established, their ships calling at both the island of St. Helena and the Cape for fresh water and what meat and produce they could procure. Two years later the rival Dutch East India Company—the V.O.C.—came into being, and through its enterprise the first white settlement was established in Southern Africa when Jan van Riebeeck landed at the Cape in 1652, on the spot where Cape Town now stands.

The Cape settlement grew in importance as trade with the East prospered, and with the passage of time its population increased. Pioneers developed the rich hinterland, which is known today as the Western

Cape. In 1795 the Cape Colony was captured by the British during the Napoleonic Wars, because of its strategic importance. The Peace of Amiens in 1802 returned the Cape to Holland, but fourteen months later France and Britain were again at war, and the Cape was reoccupied by British forces in 1806, and finally ceded to Great Britain in 1814.

In 1815 a Government sponsored monthly mail service was inaugurated between England and the Cape by fast sailing ships, leaving the Thames for the Cape before continuing onto Mauritius and finally India. The first vessel to make the voyage sailed via Madeira and Rio de Janeiro and took 114 days to reach Cape Town.

As the Cape Colony expanded along the southern and eastern seaboards, ports of call were established at Port Elizabeth and Port Natal. In 1820 the British Government sponsored an emigration scheme to develop the Eastern Cape centred on Port Elizabeth, and some 4,000 volunteers were selected to pioneer the territory east of Port Elizabeth as far as the Great Fish River. They sailed from England for Algoa Bay in the fleet of 21 chartered sailing ships, and came to be known as the 1820 Settlers.

On October 13, 1825 an historic maritime event was recorded when the first steamship arrived in Table Bay on passage to India. The arrival of the "Enterprise", flying the house flag of the East India Company, caused considerable excitement at the Cape, foreshadowing as it did the shape of things to come.

The first British steamship company to attempt to provide a scheduled service was the General Screw Steam Shipping Company, which was founded in 1848 and traded between England and Turkey. Towards the end of 1850 the company entered into a contract with the British Government to establish a regular mail service between England and the Cape, and on January 27, 1851 the auxiliary steamship "Bosphorus" arrived in Table Bay after a 40 day passage from Plymouth.

The company's initial five sailings terminated at the Cape, but by the English summer of 1852 the service was extended to India, calling at Mauritius and Ceylon en route. A number of new vessels were built for the service, but by March 1854 the cost of coal, and the monetary losses sustained through mishaps to their ships, caused the company to abandon the service.

At that time the majority of British Ocean-going steamers, other than those engaged in the North Atlantic trade, were based in Southampton. They included the Peninsular and Oriental Steam Navigation Company, whose vessels traded with the Mediterranean and the East; the Royal Mail Steam Packet Company trading with the West Indies and South America; and the General Screw Steam Shipping Company, whose vessels maintained the service to South Africa and India. All three companies enjoyed a Government subsidy in addition to their mail contracts because of the high cost of obtaining coal on the respective routes steamed by their ships. Even in England coal was scarce and was carried to the Channel ports and London from South Wales in sailing brigs.

2

With a view to accelerating supply, experiments were made in shipping coal from Wales in steamships, and the first collier expressly designed for the purpose was the "John Bowes" in 1852. This led the two leading Southampton lines, P & O and R.M.S.P., to jointly form a company specifically for this purpose, under the Chairmanship of Arthur Anderson, the P & O Chairman. Originally registered as the Southampton Steam Collier Company Ltd. the name was soon changed to the Union Steam Collier Company Ltd. and its initial board meeting was held in 1853.

Arthur Anderson was born at Lerwick in the Shetland Islands in 1792. As a young lad he joined the Royal Navy and served during the Napoleonic Wars, rising to the rank of Captain's Clerk. After the final defeat of Napoleon at Waterloo in 1815, Anderson obtained a position as a clerk to a small shipping concern. Showing a natural talent for all aspects of ships and shipping he was made a partner in the firm in 1822. The company prospered and ten years later Anderson and his senior partner Wilcox were appointed managers of a concern that was later to be known throughout the world as the P & O.

The Union Steam Collier Company ordered five colliers measuring between 380 and 530 gross tons, with a cargo capacity of 500 tons. But before they had entered service Europe was again at war.

In September 1853 Turkey declared war on Russia, and by March 1854 Great Britain had entered the conflict in support of the Turks, becoming involved for the next two years in the bitter struggle of the Crimean War. The outbreak of hostilities led to the Admiralty requisitioning all suitable British merchant shipping for employment as transport, thereby denuding the larger mail companies of the ships necessary to maintain their services. Hardest hit was the P & O whose Levant service had to be suspended, and the five colliers of the Union Company were employed to replace them. However, by March 1855 all five colliers were themselves under Government charter, and the company prospered sufficiently to acquire a sixth vessel. In 1856 though, the defeat of Russia brought the Crimean War to an end, and with six idle ships on its hands the future of the company gave cause for concern, as others were now supplying coal to Southampton.

The Board decided to open a service to Brazil, in competition to the R.M.S.P. which naturally resented this incursion into what it considered was its bailiwick. Nonetheless for the next twelve months three of the Union Company's ships were employed on the Southampton—Rio de Janeiro service. As the company was no longer engaged in ferrying coal it was reconstituted as the Union Steamship Company, Ltd., and registered as such on December 5 1856. The Brazilian service proved a costly failure, and early in 1857 it was abandoned and the fleet put out to charter, in the course of which one was lost. Fortunately in September the situation had changed for the better, for at the Annual General Meeting on October 22, 1857 Anderson informed shareholders that their company had been awarded the mail contract to Cape Town. It was an association with South Africa that was to last for 120 years, when the mail service to the Cape finally terminated in October 1977.

In 1857 South Africa was still an under-developed member of the British Empire, the only two British possessions of any consequence being the Cape Colony and Natal. Resentment at the British occupation of the Cape had led in 1836 to the departure of the Boers in the Great Trek to what were to become the Republics of the Orange Free State and Transvaal. So there appeared at the time little to attract men or money to a country so fundamentally split into two camps; a situation further aggravated by continuous Kaffir wars in both the Eastern Cape and Natal.

The Cape, by far the more important settlement, could not afford to build a breakwater, let alone a dock, and there was as yet no railway. The only exports the two Colonies had to offer were minimal amounts of wine and wool, loaded in Table Bay from lighters, as the sand bar across entrance to Port Natal limited its use to small craft only.

The failure of the first mail service to the Cape in 1854 was a severe set back to the development of trade between England and South Africa, a situation further aggravated when a second mail service, introduced by a British Member of Parliament in 1856, collapsed the following year.

The time was ripe for the Union Line to enter the mail service, and within eleven days of receiving the mail contract from the British Admiralty the "Dane" was ready to sail. In the short time available there had been little opportunity of advising the public of the vessel's departure date, and when she sailed from Southampton to inaugurate the new service she carried only six passengers and a modicum of freight in addition to the 610 tons of coal and stores required for the long voyage to the Cape.

The contract stipulated a monthly service to and from Table Bay or Simon's Bay, dependent on the weather, with the southbound mail embarked at Plymouth. The ships employed were to complete the passage both ways within 42 days, failing which penalties would be incurred, and was for an initial period of five years carrying an annual subsidy of £33,000. Finally, and of particular interest to the current service provided by the RMS "St. Helena", calls at both St. Helena and Ascension Islands were required on the homeward journey.

The "Dane" was no ocean greyhound, and with a maximum speed under steam of only seven knots she had to rely on canvas to meet the 42 day deadline. As it was, on this her maiden voyage south, she finally anchored in Table Bay 44 days out of Plymouth.

Her arrival at the Cape was quite unexpected but when the significance of her presence in the bay was grasped there was great enthusiasm.

In those early days of the mail service it was the practice of the mail-ship to remain in Table bay for about four weeks, to await the arrival of the next steamer before commencing the northbound passage. While awaiting the arrival of the "Celt" on November 27 the "Dane's" engine was overhauled, and trials carried out with better quality coal to ensure that her homeward voyage did not exceed the stipulated 42 days schedule.

The "Dane" sailed from Table bay homeward bound on the evening of November 30, in every respect a full ship. Apart from twelve passengers and cargo the vessel carried letters and newspapers, the carriage of the mail earning the Union liner the princely sum of £54! The return passage to Southampton passed without incident and was completed in 37 days, well within the contract time.

The third Union steamer to undertake the mail run was the "Norman". The purchase by the company of two larger, more powerful steamships, the "Phoebe" and the "Athens" completed the fleet, and the five vessels maintained a regular monthly service in each direction until the early 1860s.

The Union Line was held in high regard at the Cape, so much so that the Cape Legislative Assembly voted the company a bonus of £250 per day if the mail-ship completed her southbound passage within 35 days.

In Great Britain, in his annual report for 1860, the Postmaster-General commented that 'the packets which made their voyage most frequently in less than the contract, or appointed time, were those between Devonport (Plymouth) and the Cape of Good Hope, belonging to the Union Steamship Company; the next most successful Packets in this respect being those of the Cunard Line'. Praise indeed.

In 1860 the Union Line launched its first vessel specifically designed for the Cape mail and passenger trade, the "Cambrian", measuring 1,055 tons with accommodation for sixty First-Class passengers and a further forty in the 'Fore Cabin'. Rigged as a brig the "Cambrian's" engine gave her a trial speed of ten knots. She sailed for Table Bay on her maiden voyage that year.

1860 was a memorable year for South Africa, for in July Prince Alfred paid a Royal visit, arriving in Cape Town aboard HMS "Euryalus" and during his stay tipped the first truck-load of boulders on the line of what was to become the Table Bay breakwater. Ten years were to elapse before the first vessel was able to berth alongside in the Alfred Dock, named in the Prince's honour.

When the mail contract came up for renewal in December 1862 a surprise challenger emerged in a Port Elizabeth consortium known as the Diamond Line. They committed themselves to a 40 day passage via Cape Town to Algoa Bay for a subsidy considerably less than that paid to the Union Line. They had however no ships to institute their proposed service and the new contract went as previously to the Union Line for a further seven years, stipulating a monthly sailing in each direction in 38 days, with the provision for a reduction in passage time to 35 days if and when required; while the annual subsidy was reduced to an average of £19,700. The reduced passage time presented no problem, for shortly afterward the new "Saxon" completed her maiden voyage to the Cape in the record time of 31 days, while her sister-ship the "Roman" made an even faster passage a month later.

In February 1864, as envisaged in the new mail contract, this vessel extended the mail service to Port Elizabeth, while the consortium behind the Diamond Line, despite their failure to secure the mail contract, had gone ahead and ordered two 900 ton steamers, the "Eastern Province" and the "Uitenhage". The Diamond Line's challenge was short-lived. After a promising start the Line failed to live up to its reputation, gradually sailings became less frequent until terminating in 1867.

Meanwhile prospects for the Union Line improved, and with the further construction of the new mail-ships "Celt" of 1,439 tons and "Norseman" of 1,386 tons in 1866, the company began negotiations with the British Postmaster-General for the establishment of a fortnightly service to the Cape. Under the agreement reached the existing mail contract, due to expire in 1870, was extended to 1876. The new fortnightly service was inaugurated in January 1868 and represented the greatest advance the Union Line had made since entering the Cape trade eleven years earlier.

On February 28, 1868 the company suffered a serious set back with the death of its Chairman Arthur Anderson at the age of seventy-eight. His knowledge of shipping was unsurpassed, and with the Line about to encounter its fiercest competition yet on the Cape route the continued presence of such a strong personality to guide its future might well have brought about a different outcome. Anderson was succeeded as Chairman by Sir Benjamin Phillips, a former Lord Mayor of London, but lacking his predecessor's expertise.

It was sheer misfortune that immediately following the introduction of a fortnightly mail service by the Union Line it should face a period of recession. 1868 was a bad year for the farming community in South Africa and trade was virtually nil. To add to the country's misfortune came the news of the official opening of the Suez Canal, which would divert much of the shipping until then sailing via the Cape to India, Australia and the Far East.

The set back however proved temporary for diamonds were discovered at Kimberley the following year, and by 1869 South Africa was in the grip of 'Diamond Fever' The spectre of Suez was forgotten and the recession was over. Four shipping companies were advertising passages to Cape Town in addition to the Union Line catering for the flood of emigrants seeking their fortunes on the diamond fields of the Northern Cape. Three of these quickly disappeared but one remained in business and soon caused the Union Line extreme aggravation.

Despite the increased traffic to the Cape, most heavy cargoes such as mining equipment and machinery was still carried in sailing ships and so far as steamers were concerned the only company to withstand outside competition was the Union Line. However, a formidable competitor challenged them a London ship-broker George H. Payne, who had enjoyed a close association with the Cape since the 1850's.

RMS NORSEMAN (Union Line), 1865

(Nautical Photo Agency)

7

Payne's first chartered steamer inaugurated his service in 1870 but was wrecked in Algoa Bay on New Year's Day 1871. His second vessel "Beethoven" met with better fortune, and Payne formed the Cape and Natal Steam Navigation Company.

Following the death of Arthur Anderson the Union Line had adopted a policy of consolidation rather than expansion, and no new vessels were built for the next nine years. One eleven year old steamer was acquired in 1869 and three ships were lengthened to increase their cargo capacity. But competition posed by the Cape and Natal Line was very real, and their chartered steamers made speedier passages than the mail-ships, with four new steamers on order to replace chartered vessels, but before they were completed his company's fortunes changed. There were dissensions at Board level; the cost of chartering was excessive, and the Cape and Natal line found itself with insufficient funds. Nevertheless he remained determined to make his mark on the Cape run, and chartered two steamers from a London ship-owner named Currie, the "Iceland" and the "Gothland", but with inadequate financial resources his challenge failed, and Currie found himself obliged to bear the cost of the voyages.

Donald Currie was born in Greenock on September 17, 1825, the son of a 'Hairdresser and Perfumer' who subsequently established himself in Castle Place in Belfast. At the age of fourteen he returned to Greenock to work with his uncle, but three years later moved to Liverpool to work as a freight clerk for the Cunard Line.

In 1849 the repeal of restrictive Navigation Laws by both Britain and the United States was a boost for the Transatlantic trade, and Currie was sent to Le Havre and Paris to establish offices for the Cunard Line. Five years later he was back in Liverpool in a senior position with Cunard, but his ambition was to own and operate his own ships.

In 1862 he acquired an interest in the Leith, Hull and Hamburg Line, trading to Germany, Scandinavia and the Baltic. On the death of the Line's manager that same year Donald Currie became one of the largest shareholders in the company, and his brother James was appointed Manager. He thereupon severed his long association with Cunard, and with another brother David as his partner established Donald Currie and Company in Liverpool. Determined to build and operate his own ships Currie held the Cunard Line in too high regard to compete with them in the North Atlantic trade. He chose instead to trade with India, and with his many influential friends had little difficulty in securing financial backing for his new venture.

The Suez Canal was yet to open, and with the cost of coal on the long voyage via the Cape to India negating the employment of steamships on the route, Currie opted for a fleet of sailing ships. Launched from Scottish shipyards and named after castles in the British Isles, 'Currie's Calcutta Castles' as they became known were beautiful craft and fast sailers. From the beginning Currie ensured that his vessels sailed on schedule, whether with full cargoes or not, and his policy proved popular with consignors.

Despite the success of his sailing ships two developments led to their employment in a different sphere. These were the adoption by Alfred Holt in 1865 of the tandem compound steam engine, enabling steamships to undertake voyages of up to 8,500 miles without recoaling, and the opening of the Suez Canal in 1868. Consequently Currie's vessels were now routed via the Cape to Calcutta, then onto New York and back to London circumnavigating the globe. And when Currie introduced steamships into the Cape trade, his sailing ships proved invaluable in carrying Welsh Coal to Cape Town to bunker his steamers in Table Bay. Currie's entry into the Cape passenger trade in competition to the Union Line was fortuitous. His two steamers chartered to George Payne were on passage to the Cape when Payne went out of business, and Currie was obliged to accept responsibility for their voyages. He was thereupon approached by merchants engaged in the Cape trade to maintain competition to the Union Line to which he agreed. He had initially to charter steamships while new tonnage was under construction, the first of which sailed from Dartmouth on February 23, 1872. Three more chartered vessels followed before the first of his own steamers, "Westmorland" of his Liverpool and Hamburg Line, sailed for Table Bay.

Initially the new service was advertised as the London Line, to distinguish it from the Union Line based at Southampton. It was also known as the Colonial Mail Line, while at the Cape his ships were referred to as the 'Dartmouth Boats' where the 'private' mail carried in Currie's steamers was embarked, as against the official mail taken by the Union Line mailships at Plymouth. Towards the end of 1876 Donald Currie and Company, and those associated with it, formed a private company, the Castle Packets Company, which is 1881 became a public undertaking registered as the Castle Mail Packets Company Ltd.

Shortly after entering the Cape trade Currie moved his head office to Fenchurch Street in London, where he continued his association with George Payne, appointing G.H.Payne and Company loading brokers for the 'Donald Currie Line' as the new company was generally known.

The struggle for supremacy between the Union Line and Currie's Castle Line had started and although in those early days other steamship companies briefly entered the Cape trade the way was clear for the next ten years for a straight fight between Donald Currie and the Union Line.

Currie had stolen an early march on his rival by sailing his steamers three days prior to the Union Line mail ships, which left Southampton on the 10th and 26th of each month and adhered to the contract time of 37 days, while the speedier Castle Packet arrived in Table Bay some ten days ahead of the official mail, it was ironic in the circumstances that the official postage rate of a half-ounce letter by mail-ship was one shilling, when 'private mail' in the Castle Packet cost fourpence!

Throughout 1872 Currie's chartered steamers maintained their fast schedule and in October that year the first 'Castle steamer "Walmer

Castle" anchored in Table Bay. The advent of such aggressive competition appeared to have little impact on the Union Line whose only additions to their fleet were two vessels purchased from the R M S P.

However behind the scenes the Union Line was negotiating with the British Government to extend their existing mail contract, due for renewal in 1876. Their proposal to the Postmaster-General was to increase annual sailings from 24 to 26, and from January 1, 1873 to reduce the contract passage time to 30 days. The Postmaster-General recommended acceptance.

Then in June 1872, in the face of mounting political pressure to open up the East Coast of Africa, the Union Line in association with the British India Line agreed to introduce a shipping service linking Aden, Zanzibar and Cape Town,subject to the British Treasury's acceptance of their submission to extend their existing mail contract to 1880.

On October 29 the Treasury authorised the extension of the mail contract on the terms submitted, and agreed to the East Coast service in conjunction with the B.I.Line. But these negotiations had been concluded by the British Treasury without the knowledge of the Colonial authorities at the Cape, and without having the contract ratified by the British Parliament. The outcome was an investigation into the two contracts by a Select Committee of the House of Commons, who while ratifying an eight year contract for the proposed East Coast service firmly rejected any extension to the existing mail contract.

Secure in the belief that the Treasury's acceptance of their proposals was binding the Union Line had gone ahead with acquiring new tonnage, both for the extended West Coast mail service as well as for the East Coast route, while certain of the older mail-ships were re-engined, In the event they held the East Coast mail service from 1873 to 1881, but as the service is outside the scope of this book suffice it to say that when the contract expired it was not renewed and the ships were withdrawn from the Cape to Zanzibar run.

The Union Line had no illusions as to Donald Currie's intention to bid for the Cape mail contract due for renewal in 1876. For angered by the failure of the British Treasury to consult with it over their clandestine negotiations with the Union Line, the Cape Legislative Assembly exercised its inherent right to negotiate direct with Donald Currie, in order to ensure that the Castle Line would be in a position to tender against the Union Line for the new mail contract only three years away.

A significant stipulation by the Cape Parliament was that Currie was forbidden to amalgamate with the Union Line, nor would he be permitted to enter an agreement with that company to eliminate competition between them.

A seven year mail contract signed on October 5, 1876, shared equally between the Union Line and the Castle Line, was a triumph for Donald Currie, introducing as it did weekly mail service with alternate sailings by

Sir Donald Currie   (Union-Castle Line)

ships of the two concerns, while reducing the passage of time to 26 days, or 27 days when a call was included at St. Helena. No subsidy would be paid to either company who instead were to receive the total postage on such mail as their respective ships carried, while at the same time the official postage rate was reduced from one shilling to sixpence per half-ounce letter. The new contract also contained the proviso that during the currency of the seven year contract the Lines were prohibited from amalgamation without approval of the Government of the Cape Colony.

The Union Line, whose commitment had been reduced from 36 to 26 sailings annually, now had surplus vessels on its hands, and decided to launch a new monthly service between Southampton and Port Elizabeth. This was introduced in November 1876 by their liner "Syria", and came to be known as the 'Intermediate' as distinct from the mail service.

Four Castle liners capable of maintaining the new accelerated schedule were already in commission, while by 1876 they had been joined by a fifth. Four similar vessels followed, all designed to carry around 100 First Class passengers, 50 Second Class, and if necessary 100 emigrants.

The 'Donald Currie' steamers were now as well known at the Cape as those of the long established Union Line. By contrast with the black hulls, black funnels, and even black upperworks sported by the Union ships, the Castle Liners were easily distinguishable in their livery of grey hull, black-topped vermilion funnel, and dazzling white upperworks. The Castle Line also enjoyed one major advantage over its rival, which was its Chairman's ability to attract favourable publicity. Donald Currie was a born entre-preneur, whereas his Union Line counterpart maintained a much lower profile. Both socially and politically ambitious, Currie courted publicity. In the 1880 General Election he was elected to Parliament as the Liberal member for Perthshire, while on July 20 1881 he was awarded a knight-hood,and his Castle Line was launched as a public company.

In 1880 trade with South Africa flourished and both Lines were obliged to charter extra tonnage. Not only was there now room for both of them on the Cape runs but for new companies as well. Bullard, King & Company's Natal Line, whose sailing ships had linked the United King-dom with Port Natal for twenty years, introduced their first steamship into the service. Two years later a second old established Natal concern, John T. Rennie & Son, followed suit, while Clan Line entered the Cape trade with sailings from Glasgow and Liverpool, with the support of shippers located in Scotland and the Midlands for their fleet of freighters.

A year later an attempt by the Union Line Chairman Sir Benjamin Phillips to change the Line's home port from Southampton to London, to more effectively meet the competition provided by the Castle Line led to a state of turmoil. Defeat of this plan led to the inevitable resignation of March 23,1883 of Sir Benjamin Phillips and all the Directors bar Alfred Giles who was duly elected Chairman. With both Lines satisfactorily established in competition with one another, the Colonial Government

(A. Duncan)

RMS WARWICK CASTLE (Castle Line), 1877

13

had been more exacting in its requirements and less generous in its rewards. Passage time was to be reduced; while an annual subsidy to each company replaced their entitlement to the postage on all mail carried.

The entry of two more shipping companies into the Cape trade, the South African Line and the International Line, increased the number of companies participating on the Cape run to seven. Both new concerns were welcomed by the Cape Government in providing additional competition, indeed the International Line was awarded a Government contract to convey emigrants to the Cape.

This development led to Sir Donald Currie initiating a move to regulate competition between the seven, primarily designed to maintaining regular freight rates. The outcome was the formation in September 1883 of The South African Shipping Conference. A decision, some three years later, to reward shippers whose cargoes were carried exclusively in Conference Line vessels in the form of 'Deferred Rebates', was however to lead to much contention in later years. Unfortunately the formation of the Shipping Conference coincided with another recession in the South African economy which lasted for the next four years. The diamond market collapsed; the country was in the grip of a prolonged drought; and with combined exports and imports almost halved shipping was badly affected, so much so that many vessels were laid up, with the Intermediate services withdrawn by both the Union and the Castle Lines.

At the height of the recession relief was heralded when gold was discovered on the Witwatersrand, although it was not until 1889 that the vessels of the two mail-ships concerns was once again in full employment. In the circumstances it is not surprising that during this period no new construction was under-taken by either company.

In 1887 Sir Donald Currie visited South Africa to inspect the Kimberley diamond-fields and to pay courtesy calls on the presidents of the two Boer Republics. Visits to the Newcastle coal-fields in Northern Natal, and the vineyards of the Western Cape followed, while prior to his return to England Sir Donald discussed terms and conditions governing the 1888 mail contract with the Cape Government.

The development of the new gold-fields meant opportunities for emigrants to the Transvaal Republic led by an influx of Hollanders, a move warmly welcomed by President Kruger. This led to both mail-ship companies including a call at a Dutch port by their Intermediate steamers, and shortly after the Castle Line included Flushing in their sailing schedule they were awarded the contract to carry mails between the Netherlands and South Africa.

The sharp increase in demand for passenger accommodation encouraged both companies to augment their Intermediate ships. The Union Line purchased two elderly steamers which proved unsuitable, while Sir Donald Currie built two ships which came into service in 1890 and 1891. For the mail service Currie's latest and largest vessel was the 5,600 ton "Dunottar

RMS SCOT (Union Line) after lengthening, 1896   (Nautical Photo Agency)

Castle" which arrived in Table Bay on her maiden voyage on October 28, 1890, setting a new soutbound record. She represented the greatest challenge yet to the Union Line, a challenge met by their launching the twin-screw 6,844 ton liner "Scot" complete with clipper bow, twin tall slender funnels, and the graceful lines of a yacht.

The "Scot" was the first Union Line mail-ship to be painted in the new company livery of white hull, fawn upperworks and yellow funnels, a welcome change from the previous dreary black. But lovely to look at, and record-breaker that she was, the "Scot" cost a fortune in coal, while her freight capacity provided insufficient income to make her economically viable. She did however in 1893 establish a record passage to the Cape of 14 days 19 hours which stood for the next 43 years.

The development of the Witwatersrand gold-fields was so extensive that heavy machinery and equipment was being shipped from America in addition to Great Britain and the continent, and the mail ship companies introduced direct services between the United States and South Africa in 1893.

In 1892 the Bucknalls started their British and Colonial Line from the United Kingdom to South African ports, later to become so well-known as the Ellerman and Bucknall 'City' ships, while passenger traffic to and from the Cape was further eroded by steamers making round voyages from the United Kingdom via the Cape to Australia.

Furthermore homeward bound freight out of Durban was shipped almost exclusively by the two 'Direct' Lines, Bullard King's Natal Line and John T. Rennie & Son. The advent of the German East Africa Line— the D.O.A.L.—added to their problem, for by 1894 German steamers were circumnavigating the African continent in both directions. Their vessels outward bound provided strong competition to the Intermediate ships of both the Union and the Castle Lines' sailing from, Continental ports; and to keep them under some measure of control in the regulation of passenger fares and freight rates, Sir Donald Currie succeeded in the autumn of 1894 in persuading the D.O.A.L. Chairman Adolph Woermann to join the South African Shipping Conference.

Sir Donald visited the Cape again in 1893 to negotiate a new mail contract continuing the mail service until 1900 under the same terms and conditions then prevailing, except that the passage time was cut to 19 days. When this new mail contract came into operation in late 1893 the Union Line was again in financial difficulties. The Chairman Alfred Giles blamed the high cost of coal; but other views blamed the Board for lack of foresight and bad management. In the final outcome illness forced the resignation of Alfred Giles in 1894. He was replaced as Chairman by his Deputy, Sir Francis Evans, a Civil Engineer turned banker, with a reputation of being a capable businessman.

Following the death of Alfred Giles the vacancy on the Board was filled by Gustav Wolff, a partner in the ship-building firm Harland and Wolff, and thereafter all the Union ships were built at Belfast. But before Wolff joined the Board William Pirrie, a partner in Harland and Wolff, visited South Africa to study local conditions and design ships to meet the particular needs of the Cape Trade. The result was a new class of Intermediate ship of modest speed, a large cargo capacity, and saloon accommodation in three classes for around 200 passengers. Eventually ten were built. With twin screws and a light draught they could berth alongside at Durban and East London, a great advantage over previous ships of similar size.

William Pirrie had been responsible for the design of the famous White Star transatlantic liners, and his next commission for the Union Line was a new mail-ship, with accommodation well in advance of anything previously seen on the Cape run. The result was the twin-screw beautifully proportioned two-funnelled 7,500 ton "Norman".

Donald Currie had nothing to compete with the "Norman", adding two single-screw steamers some 2,000 tons smaller with inferior facilities, and six sub-standard Intermediates.

In 1896 the Castle line experienced its greatest set-back since entering the Cape Trade. For almost 25 years their steamers had made their round voyages without loss of life, but in June their "Drummond Castle" homeward bound was wrecked off Ushant and of the 245 on board only three survived.

By 1897 the future of the Union Line looked much better following the success of the new Intermediates, and the mail-ship "Norman" on the Cape run. Furthermore their famous "Scot" had been lengthened to carry extra cargo and additional passengers and was now sailing less unprofitably.

Not until the launch of the sister-ships "Kinfauns Castle" and "Kildonan Castle" in 1899 did Sir Donald Currie match the mail-ships built by Harland and Wolff for his rival. Twin-screw liners measuring 9,660 tons, the two new Castle ships incorporated many features pioneered by the Union Line.

The mail contract came up for renewal in 1900, and somewhat surprisingly the Cape Government announced that the contract would be put out to tender, and would be awarded to a single concern. Neither the Union nor the Castle Line wished to compete with one another, for had they done so the successful tenderer would have needed to build or purchase four or five additional vessels. So neither submitted a tender, and in fact no tenders were received, so the Cape Government had no option but to agree to the Union and the Castle line sharing the new mail contract as before. The same terms and conditions as in the 1893 contract applied, with one notable exclusion. The clause denying the two companies the right to amalgamate was omitted and Sir Donald Currie took immediate steps to seek an amicable arrangement acceptable to both companies.

In December 1899 Currie realised his ambition when the Boards of the two companies agreed to merge their interests, and to consolidate their

17

(A. Duncan)

SS GASCON (Union Line), 1897

two fleets into a single concern. At meetings held on February 13, 1900 the shareholders of the respective Lines approved the take-over and from the Union Line fleet comprising 114,000 tons, and the Castle ships totalling 107,000 tons, emerged a fleet second to none.

On March 8, 1900 the Union Castle Mail Steamship Company Ltd was registered, and the immediate effect on the ships of the Union Line was a change in their livery to that of their ertswhile rivals, although the vessels retained their names. Clearly Sir Donald Currie had dominated the negotiations and the Union Line had lost its identity.

Under the Chairmanship of Sir Donald Currie the Union-Castle Line appointed Donald Currie and Company to manage the new concern with Sir Francis Evans becoming a partner.

II   THE RISE AND DECLINE IN THE CAPE PASSENGER TRADE: 1900–1977

The first of the Union-Castle Mail Steamship Company's ships to sail from Southampton under the new company house-flag was the "Dunottar Castle" on March 17, 1900. Curiously the Union Line had been founded in 1853 under the threat of war in the Crimea, and almost fifty years later the new Union-Castle Line came into being under the shadow of the Second Boer War.

Hostilities between the Boers and the British commenced in mid-October 1899, and while the regular weekly sailings of the mail-ships continued as before, the Intermediate service was disrupted by the requirements of the Admiralty to move troops and supplies to the Cape, when five of the steamers employed in that service were requisitioned.

When war had appeared inevitable the Johannesburg offices of both Lines closed by the beginning of October, but not before the two Agents had negotiated passages home for the hundreds of British miners and engineers intent on leaving the country. In all, between July and December 1899 14,700 persons were carried back to the United Kingdom.

The Natal coal mines ceased production as the Boers fought their way south to Ladysmith, and because the steamers of both companies had relied on supplies of Natal coal at their Durban terminal, vast stocks had to be shipped to the Cape from the Welsh coal-fields, adding to congestion already created by the mass of shipping conveying both private and Government cargoes to the port.

The weekly departure of the mail-ships was however jeopardised by the loss of the "Tantallon Castle" on Robben Island in May 1901, following that of the "Mexican" the previous year. With the loss of two of the regular mail-ships the weekly sailings could only be maintained by terminating outward voyages at Port Elizabeth, with a feeder service to Durban provided by one of the Intermediate steamers not requisitioned for Government service.

On May 31, 1902 the unhappy conflict ended, and in August three distinguished Boer Generals led by Louis Botha sailed for England in the Union-Castle liner "Saxon" to seek British assistance for their defeated countrymen.

This is a convenient moment to consider other participants using the Cape route. While the Union-Castle Line was by far the most important company to be engaged on the Cape run, it should not be forgotten that the steamships of Alfred Holt's Blue Funnel Line had been calling at Table Bay on passage to Australia and the Far East since 1865; and in the previous chapter mention was made of the German East Africa Line, or D.O.A.L., calling at the Cape en route to Tanganyika.

There was also the Bucknall Line, while vessels of the Aberdeen—White Star Line, and those of the Shaw, Savill and Albion Line were regular visitors to the Cape on their way to Australia before the turn of the century. Further competition for the passenger trade had been generated by the advent of the Woermann Line, a German company also engaged in the East Africa service linking Tanganyika with the Fatherland; and soon in 1906 the Portugese were to make their presence felt, when the Empreza Nacional de Navegacao introduced a service out of Lisbon. Their ships called at Angola on the west coast of Africa and terminated their voyages at Mocambique calling at South African ports both outward and homeward bound.

Meanwhile prospects at the end of hostilities had raised hopes of post-war prosperity, which the Union-Castle Line anticipated by acquiring ten freighters to take advantage of the expected increase in trade, six designed especially to carry the influx of immigrants envisaged. The boom failed to materialise and these ships instead were employed on the America-South Africa run, or on a monthly service between the United Kingdom and Mauritius.

Despite this, new tonnage was needed for the mail and intermediate services. For the latter three ships were constructed to an entirely new design and provided highly successful, while two 13,000 ton mail-ships emerged at the same time.

Despite the recession the Houston Line made a bid for the freight trade to the Cape by undercutting the Conference Lines. Not until January 1904 did Houston agree to join the South African Shipping Conference.

By 1905, apart from the weekly mail-ship which left Southampton for the Cape every Saturday, Intermediate steamers sailed each week from London on Fridays, and from Southampton every Saturday. The Intermediates called at the Canary Islands, and once a month at Ascension, St. Helena and Delagoa Bay.

Sir Francis Evans died unexpectedly in 1907, and his son Murland succeeded to the title and took his father's place as a partner in Donald Currie and Company. Now 82, Sir Donald Currie still took an active interest in the affairs of the Line, in particular with regard to negotiations for the new mail contract due to come into force during 1910. His company was the only one to respond to the invitation to submit tenders for the new contract called for in 1908, but as the respective South African Governments were engaged in discussions leading to the Union of the four territories, a decision on awarding the contract was held in abeyance.

Confident that the mail contract would be renewed, Sir Donald Currie proceeded with the construction of two new liners for the mail service, the "Balmoral Castle " and "Edinburgh Castle", similar in size and appearance to the earlier "Armadale Castle" and "Kenilworth Castle"; as well

RMS BALMORAL CASTLE (Union-Castle Line), 1910

(A. Duncan)

as two new Intermediates. They were the last four ships he was to order for he died at Sidmouth in Devon on April 13, 1909 in his 84th year. He was succeeded as Chairman and senior partner of the Management Company by his son-in-law Frederick Mirrielees.

In 1910 the formal union of the four self-governing colonies of the Cape, Natal, the Transvaal and the Orange Free State was ratified, and the Union of South Africa came into being. The first Governor-General, Lord Gladstone took office in April that year, while the first Union Parliament was formally opened by the Duke of Connaught in October.

The following year Percy Molteno of the Union-Castle line arrived at the Cape to finalise the new mail contract with the Minister of Posts and Telegraphs, Sir David Graaff, only to learn that no company applying the Rebate System would be awarded the contract, and negotiations between Molteno and the Government broke down.

When fresh tenders for the contract were called for the Union-Castle Line, as a member of the South African Shipping Conference, was pre-cluded from responding, while no satisfactory tender was received from other Lines. An impasse had been reached, for neither the Government nor the Union-Castle Line would give way, but as the current contract had been extended into 1912 there was still time for concessions.

The breakdown in the negotiations left Union-Castle in a vulnerable position. In December an offer of £32.10.0 per £10 share was made for the Company and in April 1912 the new owners took over, 40 years after Donald Currie entered the Cape trade, marking the end of a long chapter in the history of the Line.

Control of the Union-Castle Mail Steamship Company had been acquired by Sir Owen Phillips, Chairman of the Royal Mail Steam Packet Company. Undoubtedly Lord Pirrie, whose knowledge of the company's operations and potential dated back to his close association with the ex-Union Line twenty years previously, had advised his friend and colleague of the situation, for he had previously acted in a similar capacity when Sir Owen acquired Elder Dempster Lines. Unsurprisingly Lord Pirrie was immediately appointed to the Board of the Union-Castle Line.

Sir Owen Phillips was in the process of building up a vast shipping empire, having already taken over both the Glen and Shire Lines in 1907, and the Pacific Steam Navigation Company three years later. His new acquisition cost the R.M.S.P., in association with Elder Dempster Lines, something over £5 million, but other than the change in ownership and the management of the Line, there were no immediate changes of any consequence.

Immediately Sir Owen Phillips advised the South African Government that Union-Castle were prepared to resign from the South African Shipping Conference, thereby opening the way to negotiating the new mail contract, and he was invited to visit the Cape to conclude a settlement. But before departing Sir Owen authorised the construction of the two Intermediate

SS GUILDFORD CASTLE (Union-Castle Line), 1911

(A. Duncan)

steamers necessary to improve the new East Coast service which had been inaugurated in 1910.

The new mail contract was far reaching, covering as it did commitments to bunkering the vessels of the fleet; providing for the conveyance of perishable freight; and preferential rates for the carriage of agricultural products and pedigree livestock, as well as Government equipment and materials. Passage time for the mail-ships was cut to 16 days 15 hours; all rebates were abolished; while six new mail -ships were required to be built during the currency of the ten year agreement, each of not less than 15,000 tons.

However, only two years after the new contract had come into force Great Britain and Germany were at war, disrupting the mail-ship sailings and causing the Intermediate service to be abandoned in its entirety. Within a month of the commencement of hostilities 19 of the company's 41 vessels had been requisitioned for Government service, but by employing Intermediate steamers, on the mail run a reasonably regular weekly sailing was maintained for the next two years. Ultimately the company lost 8 Intermediate and cargo ships by enemy action.

It was a long time before Union-Castle were able to resume a full normal service. Not only were the company's ships employed in the repatriation of troops and civilians to Australasia, South Africa, and to other parts of the British Empire but after four years of trooping and hard steaming the liners needed overhaul and reconditioning. No mail-ships had been lost, and the 19,000 ton "Arundel Castle", which had been laid down in 1915, and her sister-ship "Windsor Castle", eventually came into service in 1921 and 1922 respectively. By October 1919 the regular mail service had been resumed, but only in 1922 was the Intermediate service reintroduced on a reduced but regular basis.

During the 1920s the problems facing the Union- Castle Line were compounded by the sharp increase in competition for the passenger trade between the United Kingdom and the Continent, both to and from South Africa and East Africa, as new lines emerged to claim a share of this lucrative market in the post war era, with the Bucknall Line controlled by Sir John Ellerman eventually proved to be Union-Castle's greatest rivals on the Cape run.

Likewise a number of Dutch passenger liners entered the Cape trade in the immediate post-war period, reaching prominence in 1922 when they merged to become the Holland-Africa Line. By 1922 the pre-war services between Germany, South West Africa and Tanganyika undertaken by the D.O.A.L. and Woermann were resumed, with the two companies now merged to become the German-Africa Lines; Bullard King's Natal Line, a Union-Castle subsidiary since 1919, acquired two inferior vessels from Union-Castle to augment their passenger trade in 1924; and the Italian Navigazione Libera Triestina began a service to the Cape a year later. Portugal was represented by the Empresa Nacional de Navagazao, linking Lisbon with Angola and Mocambique.

SS ULYSSES (Blue Funnel Line), 1913

(World Ship Society)

Yet another slice of the passenger market was taken by the Blue Funnel Line, alternating sailings to Australia via the Cape with the Aberdeen— White Star Line; while in 1930 a second Portugese shipping company, Compania Colonial de Navagazao was carrying passengers via the Cape and Durban to Portugal's African colonies.

These activities posed little threat to the Union-Castle Line mail-ships, but with a comfortable if somewhat slower voyage on offer at cheaper prices, they did provide the Intermediate steamers with stiff competition.

But to return to the fortunes of the Union-Castle Line and its Chairman Sir Owen Phillips. The mail contract was due to expire in 1922, but post-war stresses led to its extension sine die with certain modifications.

In the New Year Honours of 1923 a Baronetcy for his services to British shipping was conferred on Sir Owen Phillips, and he assumed the title of Lord Kylsant of Carmarthen. This led to his Royal Mail Group, of which of course the Union-Castle Line was an important entity, to be commonly referred to thereafter as the Kylsant Group.

In 1926 the first motor-vessel to join the mail fleet was the 20,000 ton "Carnarvon Castle", which sailed on her maiden voyage in August. Two Intermediate motor-ships followed in 1929 and 1930, both similar versions of the new mail-ship.

By 1927 exports of perishable freight from South Africa had shown a substantial increase beyond available shipping capacity, prompting Union-Castle and the South African Government to sign a ten year freight contract in which the company guaranteed to provide the necessary additional refrigerated space. It came into force on January 1, 1929. Partly to meet the requirements of this new contract, two further improved "Carnarvon" type motor-ships were ordered, and the "Winchester Castle" and "Warwick Castle" joined the mail service in 1930 and 1931 respectively.

Although by 1920 Lord Kylsant presided over an enormous shipping complex, he was determined to expand it even further, gaining control of a number of well-known concerns, culminating in the purchase in 1927 of the famous White Star Line, after which control of the Australian Commonwealth Line and the Shaw Savill and Albion Line soon followed.

Apart from these expensive acquisitions Lord Kylsant had long committed his Group to an extensive building programme financed by the British Government. It soon became apparent that these acquisitions, in particular that of the White Star Line, had been ill-timed, for by 1929 the world had entered into a period of extreme depression. Millions of tons of shipping were laid up, while the Kylsant Group were obligated to repay the loans made to it by the British Treasury to finance their extensive building programme.

When the British Government refused to extend the period for repayment, Lord Kylsant was forced to raise the necessary funds by the issue of Debenture Stock in the Group's parent company, The Royal Mail

Owen Philipps (Lord Kylsant) c. 1904

(The Hon. Mrs. N. D. Fischer Hoch)

Steam Packet Company. Subsequently it was alleged that the prospectus relative to the issue was fraudulent, in that the unspecified transfer of taxation reserves no longer required to the trading account gave an inaccurately favourable impression to would-be investors of the company's profitability, whereas in fact the R.M.S.P. had been trading unprofitably for several years. In May 1931 Lord Kylsant was charged with publishing a false prospectus. He was found guilty and imprisoned, an unnecessarily harsh sentence for what was basically an accountancy technicality. His imprisonment cost him his Directorship on the Boards of 41 companies, 36 of which he had become Chairman. On his release Lord Kylsant retired to his home in South Wales where he died on June 7, 1937.

On the collapse of the Kylsant empire, Robertson Gibb, who had joined the staff of the Union Line as far back as 1883, was elected Chairman of the Union-Castle Line, with Sir Vernon Thomson Deputy Chairman. The financial problems facing the Line following the break-up of the Kylsant Group were serious, and it was not until 1936 that the company was able to fully rehabilitate its finances.

In 1933 Lloyd Triestino caused the Union-Castle Line irritation by introducing two 19 knot Transatlantic liners to the Cape trade. Despite the variation in tonnage, the 23,600 ton "Duilio" and 21,900 ton "Giulio Cesare" were sister-ships, and not only were they far more luxurious than any vessel in the Union-Castle fleet, but they were also three knots faster than the mail-ships. Lloyd Triestino had negotiated a five year contract with the South African Government to carry the mail to and from Italy, which gave rise to misgivings concerning the renewal of the British mail contract in the Union-Castle Boardroom. However, when the Italian mail contract expired in 1938, and was not renewed by the South African authorities, both liners were withdrawn from the Cape trade.

The Union-Castle Board decided to counter the Italian initiative by building the motor-ships "Stirling Castle" and "Athlone Castle" which joined the mail-ship fleet in 1936, followed by the slightly larger "Capetown Castle" two years later. Not only did these three new liners offer improved passenger accommodation, they matched the Italian ships for speed.

In 1936 the Union-Castle Chairman Robertson Gibb visited the Cape to negotiate a new mail contract to come into force on January 1, 1937 for a ten year period. In terms of this agreement the Line committed itself to a passage time of 14 days for the mail-ships, to become effective from January 1, 1939. The three day reduction in passage time necessitated re-engining five of the current mail-ships with, in three instances, partial hull reconstruction. All five liners underwent their refits at Harland and Wolff's yard at Belfast, and on their return to the mail service were also greatly improved in outward appearance.

To maintain the existing mail service while the five mail-ships were modernised, two 15,000 ton Intermediates, "Dunnottar Castle" and "Dunvegan Castle" joined the fleet in 1936 and two 'improved' ships of the same class were ordered the following year.

RMS WINDSOR CASTLE (Union-Castle Line) as built, 1922

(World Ship Society)

RMS ARUNDEL CASTLE (Union-Castle Line) after rebuilding, 1937　　　(A. Duncan)

RMMV CARNARVON CASTLE (Union-Castle Line) as rebuilt, 1950   (World Ship Society)

After 55 years service, initially with the Union Line and subsequently the Union-Castle Line, Robertson Gibb retired as Chairman in 1939. He was succeeded by Sir Vernon Thomson who was immediately faced with the complete dislocation of the mail service following the outbreak of World War II in September that year.

During the 1930s Ellerman Lines introduced some 12 "Cities" into the Cape trade. All were 8,000 to 10,000 tons with a service speed of 12 knots, and carried passengers initially in two classes, but later in one class only. Comfortable, with relatively low fares, the "Cities" proved very popular, and became Union-Castle Line's main opposition.

At the end of the First World War Alfred Holt's Blue Funnel Line had five ships sailing from Liverpool for Australian ports via Cape Town and Durban. This service they shared with the Aberdeen-White Star Line, later to be absorbed into the Shaw, Savill and Albion Line.

During the 1930s four more passenger ships were employed on the Australian run, but of the total of nine vessels five were lost in the course of the Second World War. The four survivors, the steamships "Ascanius", "Nestor", "Sarpedon" and "Antenor", continued to sail via South African ports until the early 1950s. Somewhat dated in design and passenger facilities, and with an optimistic service speed of 14 knots, the "Ascanius" and the "Nestor", along with the "Anchises" and "Ulysses" which did not survive the war, had the enviable reputation of being 'happy' ships, and they attracted many 'regulars' on the passage between the United Kingdom and South Africa, or between South Africa and Australia.

Between the two World Wars the Aberdeen-White Star Line and the Aberdeen and Commonwealth Line operated ten ships on the Australia run via the Cape under the same management. But in 1932 both fleets were acquired by the Shaw, Savill and Albion Line, and for the remainder of their days in service wore that company's livery and flew its house-flag.

Best known and best loved of these were the 11,000 ton "Themistocles" and the 18,700 ton "Ceramic", lost to enemy action in the South Atlantic in 1942, when all but one of the 656 on board perished.

Bullard King's Natal Line augmented their passenger trade in 1924 with two ex-Union-Castle ships renamed "Umkuzi" and "Umvoti". Measuring 5,200 tons with a service speed of 10.5 knots they sailed between London and Durban as one-class ships until withdrawn from service in 1938 and 1940. Between 1935 and 1938 the Line launched three sister-ships "Umtata", "Umtali" and "Umgeni". These coal-fired 8,150 ton steamships carried 100 one-class passengers in well designed, comfortable but unostentatious accommodation; and with a service speed of 13 knots proved popular with ocean travellers to and from Africa.

The German Africa Lines re-entered the passenger trade between the Continent and East Africa via South West Africa and South African ports in 1919, and provided a service that proved immensely successful right up to the outbreak of the Second World War.

SS DUILIO (Lloyd Triestino), 1923

(Dr E. Cornish collection)

SS WATUSSI (Woermann/DOA Lines), 1928   (Robert Pabst collection)

RMMV WINCHESTER CASTLE (Union-Castle Line) as built, 1930 (World Ship Society)

RMMV ATHLONE CASTLE (Union-Castle Line), 1936   World Ship Society

SS UMTATA (Natal Line), 1935

(A. Duncan)

MV DOMINION MONARCH (Shaw Savill Line), 1939

(A. S. Mallett collection)

The initial three passenger ships to enter the post First World War service were the sister-ships "Usaramo", "Ussakuma" and "Wangoni" all measuring 7,900 tons with a service speed of 13 knots. All three vessels were either sunk or taken as prizes by the Allied Forces during World War II. They were joined in 1922 by the 4,700 ton sister-ships "Wadai" and "Wahehe", and in 1923–1924 by the larger, faster steamers "Adolph Woermann", "Usambara", "Njassa" and "Tanganyika", all measuring about 8,700 tons with a service speed of 14 knots.

The growing popularity of the Line can be gauged by the transfer to the Africa service from the North Atlantic trade in 1926 of the 8,100 ton "Toledo", but during the world depression in 1930 she was withdrawn from the Africa run and laid up.

A new departure for the D.O.A.L. and the Woermann Line, constituting the German Africa Lines, was the construction of two steamships measuring 9,500 tons with a service speed of 16 knots. Carrying passengers in three classes the "Watussi" and "Ubena" came into service in 1928 and were very popular ships with the travelling public. The "Watussi" was scuttled south of Cape Point in December 1939 when intercepted by the South African Air Force, but the "Ubena" survived the Second World War; was awarded to Great Britain as part of the war reparations, and served as a peacetime troopship under management of the Royal Mail Line until scrapped in 1957.

The last two passenger liners to be built for the German Africa Lines were the well-proportioned "Pretoria" and "Windhuk". These two steamships joined the Line in 1937, and measuring 16,662 tons with a service speed of 17.5 knots established an excellent reputation for service, comfort and cuisine in the brief period they were on the Cape run, before the outbreak of World War II two years later. Both survived the conflict, the "Pretoria" going to Great Britain to become the troopship "Empire Orwell" while the "Windhuk" was taken over by the United States as a naval transport.

Earlier in this chapter brief mention was also made of the Portugese Empreza Nacional de Navegacao, which until 1930 had a monopoly on the sea route linking Portugal with Angola and Mocambique. Although the company had been in the passenger trade since 1906, their first two liners of any significance were the 6,300 ton "Lourenco Marques" and the 9,000 ton "Nyassa". Both vessels were German prizes, seized by the Portugese when they entered the First World War on the side of the Allies in 1916. They entered service with the company, reconstituted in 1918 as the National Navigation Company, when the war was over and were only scrapped in 1951 and 1952 respectively.

To counter the competition posed by the advent of a second Portugese company, the Colonial Navigation Company, which commenced operations on the same route in 1930, the National Navigation Company built the 6,500 ton "Quanza", and purchased in 1933 the Belgian "Albertville" which was renamed "Angola". The "Angola" was scrapped in 1952 after 40 years service, while "Quanza" was of a similar vintage when sold for scrap in 1968.

December 1919 saw the entry of Dutch shipping into the Cape passenger trade with the formation of the Holland-Africa Line. The service from the Continent to East Africa via South West Africa and the Cape was launched by the chartered "Rijndijk", soon followed by the first of the "Fonteins". Three modern 6,000 ton steamers had been purchased by the new Line and renamed "Jagersfontein", "Rietfontein" and "Randfontein".

The first cargo-liners specifically designed and built for the Cape trade were the 5,500 ton "Klipfontein" and the 6,400 ton "Springfontein". Both vessels offered accommodation for 34 passengers, and their advent raised the company's fleet to six, then to seven following the purchase of the 6,000 ton "Cedario" renamed "Meliskerk".

By 1932 competition from the German Africa Lines, added to the effect of the world trade recession, saw the Holland-Africa Line in financial difficulties, and the company went into liquidation. Its fleet and service were bought by the United Netherlands Navigation Company, who instituted a two-way round Africa service restyled the Holland-Afrika Lijn.

In 1934 the 7,100 ton "Nieukerk" was transferred to the Holland-Afrika Lijn flag, and was joined by two new motor-ships, the 10,000 ton sisters "Bloemfontein" and "Jagersfontein". These three vessels, all with improved passenger facilities, replaced the original "Rietfontein", "Klipfontein" and the early "Jagersfontein", and proved to be very popular ships.

The last of the shipping companies to provide a passenger link between the Continent and South Africa was the Lloyd Triestino Line sailing from Italy. Started in 1925 as the Navigazione Libera Triestina, for the first five years the company operated a round-Africa service via Suez and the East African coast, returning home via the Cape and West Africa. In 1930 this service was complemented by sailings down the west coast of Africa outward bound, and home via the Cape, East African ports, and the Suez Canal.

Four steamers of 5,500 tons maintained the round-Africa service for the Navigazione Libera Triestina Line for the first seven years, the "Maiella", "Perla", "Sabbia" and "Sistiana". Unostentatious vessels that they were they did provide comfortable passenger accommodation and good cuisine, but at the painfully slow service speed of 10 knots. None were to survive World War II. They had been joined in 1932 by the larger, faster "Leme" of 8,100 tons, and capable of 14 knots, but the "Leme" did not return to the Cape in the post-war period.

With the establishment in 1930 of the complementary round-Africa service more vessels were required. This resulted in four 12 knot cargo-liners joining the fleet, the "Duchess D'Aosta", "Piave", "Timavo" and "Rosandra", all measuring between 7,500 and 8,000 tons. Once again none of these four ships survived the Second World War.

Sir Vernon Thomson and Field Marshall Jan Smuts aboard PRETORIA
CASTLE, 1948   (Union-Castle Line)

The Navigazione Libera Triestina was taken over by Lloyd Triestino in the early 1930s, when their 8,000 ton liner "Gerusalemme" increased the combined fleet on the round-Africa service to ten ships. With above average accommodation, and a reputation for splendid service and cuisine, the "Gerusalemme" proved most popular.

The vital role played by the Union-Castle fleet during the conflict is not relevant to this account of the Cape passenger trade. Suffice it to say that the fleet rendered sterling service as fast troopships; as armed merchant cruisers; and in one case as an escort carrier. The only company steamer to maintain a passenger service to the Cape was the 28 year old 8,000 ton Intermediate "Gloucester Castle", until she was attacked and sunk by the German raider "Michel" in July 1942.

Immediately the war in Europe had ended in August 1945 a new mail contract was entered into by the Union-Castle Line, to come into force on January 2, 1947. In all 13 of the company's ships had been lost in the course of the war, including the mail-ships "Warwick Castle" and "Windsor Castle", and once construction commenced of the two 28,700 ton mailships to replace them, the "Pretoria Castle" and "Edinburgh Castle".

The mail service did not return to normal until the end of 1950 as three of the mail-ships were employed by the South African Government on a sponsored immigration service until May 1949, following which they underwent extensive refits.

In the early post-war years there was a spirit of optimism both in South and East Africa. The Orange Free State gold-fields had been discovered in 1946, while the British Government's groundnut scheme on a gigantic scale was expected to boost the economy of both Kenya and Tanganyika. This led to the construction of four new Intermediates, the "Bloemfontein Castle", and the three sister-ships "Rhodesia Castle", "Kenya Castle" and "Braemar Castle", all of which joined the fleet between 1950 and 1952.

Turning to the other Lines, of the Ellerman ships, when normal passenger traffic resumed post-war, the pre-war "City of Exeter", "City of Paris", "City of Canterbury" and "City of Hong Kong" kept their houseflag flying in the Cape trade until new vessels could replace them. In the early 1950s they ordered four new motor-ships which came into service between 1952 and 1954. Measuring 13,350 tons with a service speed of 16 knots the "City of Port Elizabeth", "City of York", "City of Exeter" and "City of Durban" took only 16 days for the voyage from London to Cape Town.

Their passenger accommodation and the service provided were of the highest standard, and the four ships were extremely popular with the South African public. It is a matter for sincere regret that in 1971 these lovely ships were withdrawn without replacement and sold.

Bullard King lost their "Umtata" by enemy action in 1942, but the "Umtali" and "Umgeni" resumed service after the war until 1957, when they were sold to Elder Dempster Lines. The remainder of the Natal Line's

RMS EDINBURGH CASTLE (Union-Castle Line), 1948

fleet of cargo ships were disposed of to the newly formed Springbok Line, which in turn was shortly afterwards acquired by the South African Marine Corporation, and after 100 years in the Cape trade the Natal Line went out of business.

The four Blue Funnel steamships that survived the war were joined by eight 10,000 ton passenger ships of the "Hector" and "Perseus" classes, but these ships only called at the Cape and Durban outward bound, returning home via either Suez or Panama. In accordance with company policy they were withdrawn from the passenger trade in 1965, although they continued as freighters until 1973.

The elderly Shaw, Savill "Akaroa", "Mataroa" and "Tamaroa" all survived the Second World War but were retired between 1954 and 1957. The five Aberdeen and Commonwealth Line ships taken over by Shaw, Savill in 1932 were the 14,000 ton "Arawa", "Esperance Bay", "Largs Bay", "Moreton Bay" and "Jervis Bay". The latter vessel was commissioned as an armed merchant cruiser in the Second World War and was lost in action. The four survivors returned to the Australia run after the war, but were withdrawn from service and scrapped between 1955 and 1957.

The pride of the Shaw, Savill fleet was the 27,000 ton "Dominion Monarch". A motor-ship with a service speed of 19 knots the "Dominion Monarch" sailed on her maiden voyage in mid-1939. She was soon requisitioned and served as a troopship and cargo carrier for the next eight years, only returning to normal service via the Cape in December 1948. She was withdrawn from service in 1962 and broken up in Japan.

In 1947 Shaw, Savill ordered four cargo-liners for the Australian trade, some using the Cape route, the "Athenic", "Gothic", "Ceramic" and "Corinthic", measuring around 15,000 tons. All four ceased carrying passengers in 1965, and were broken up between 1968 and 1972. In 1955 the Line introduced a one-class ship of revolutionary design, the 20,000 ton "Southern Cross", which circumnavigated the globe via the Cape to Australia and home through the Panama Canal. She was joined by the 24,000 ton "Northern Star" of similar design, which circumnavigated the globe in the opposite direction, sailing via Panama outward bound and home via the Cape. For a time this round-the-world service proved popular, and the "Akaroa", "Arawa" and "Aranda" joined the "Southern Cross" and "Northern Star" in 1969. Prior to their acquisition they had sailed for nine years in the South American trade, under the Royal Mail house-flag.

The "Southern Cross" was withdrawn from service in 1971 and sold to Greek shipping interests; the three ex-Royal Mail liners were sold in 1972 to Norwegian owners; while in 1975 the "Northern Star" was scrapped when still a comparatively new vessel.

When Italy joined the Axis in 1940 the "Gerusalemme" took refuge in neutral Lourenco Marques, and following Italy's surrender in 1943 she

SS BRAEMAR CASTLE (Union-Castle Line), 1952

(World Ship Society)

MV CITY OF YORK (Ellerman Lines), 1954   (A. S. Mallett collection)

47

was taken over by the Allies and converted into a hospital ship. Released to Lloyd Triestino when the war had ended in 1945, the "Gerusalemme" was employed only on the East Africa service via the Suez Canal as far as Durban, returning to Italy over the same route, until she was withdrawn and scrapped in 1952.

Immediately after the war the 23 year old "Toscana", a 9,600 ton cargo-liner previously operated by Lloyd Triestino on the Italy-Australia run, reopened the passenger service between Italy and the Cape. The "Toscana" sailing down the west coast complemented the "Gerusalemme", and these two vessels filled the gap until two new motor-ships under construction were ready to replace them in 1952.

The sister-ships "Africa" and "Europa" measured 11,400 tons, and were even an improvement on the high standard set by the "Duilio" and "Giulio Cesare". Designed for a service speed of 19.5 knots they were very popular ships, but the rising cost of oil fuel rendered these predominantly passenger ships uneconomical, and by 1976 both vessels were withdrawn and sold.

Holland-Afrika Lijn lost the second "Jagersfontein" through enemy action in 1942, but the "Boschfontein" (ex-"Nieukerk") returned to the Cape trade when the war had ended. From 1950 however her schedule was changed, sailing from Rotterdam only as far south as Beira in Mocambique via the Suez Canal. The "Bloemfontein" remained on the Cape run until 1959 when she was scrapped.

In 1939 "Klipfontein" had been completed and in 1950 her sister-ships "Jagersfontein" and "Oranjefontein" joined the fleet. Launched in 1940, but only completed for the Africa service after the war was over, these 10,550 ton vessels had a service speed of 17 knots, and passengers were carried in two classes, First and Tourist. The "Klipfontein" was wrecked off the coast of Mocambique in 1953, but her two sisters continued in the Africa trade until 1967 when the depressed state of the passenger market led to their withdrawal from service to be sold as scrap.

In 1958 a new 18,700 ton "Randfontein", with a service speed of 18 knots, replaced both the "Boschfontein" and the wrecked "Klipfontein", and when the "Bloemfontein" was scrapped the following year the "Randfontein" continued on the Cape run with the "Jagerfontein" and "Oranjefontein" until the latter two vessels were disposed of in 1967. Thereafter the "Randfontein" continued on the Cape run on her own until 1971, when she was sold to the Royal Interocean Line for service in the Far East, and the Holland-Afrika Lijn passenger service was abandoned.

The Portugese Lines, not being combatants, were more fortunate, but by the end of the Second World War only the "Quanza" was a relatively new vessel, and the National Navigation Company ordered two new liners to be built in the United Kingdom, with accommodation of a far superior standard to anything the company had previously provided. The new "Angola" of 13,000 tons had a service speed of 17 knots and became operational in 1948, while her sister-ship "Mocambique" joined her a year

MV EUROPA (Lloyd Triestino), 1952

(R. Pabst)

MV RANDFONTEIN (Holland Africa Line), 1958

(R. Pabst)

(R. Pabst)

SS PATRIA (Companhia Colonial de Navegacao), 1947

SS PRINCIPE PERFEITO (Companhia Nacional de Navegacao), 1961

(R. Pabst)

later. Very popular with South Africans, particularly for East Coast cruises, both vessels were withdrawn and scrapped in 1972 when, prior to Angola and Mocambique gaining their Independence, trade to the two Portugese colonies had slumped.

The last passenger liner to be built for the National Navigation Company was also their largest and fastest. The imposing and handsome "Principe Perfeito" measuring 19,400 tons with a service speed of 20 knots, was built in England and entered service in 1961. Fully air-conditioned and stabilised she set a high standard in passenger comfort, but like the "Angola" and "Mocambique" was withdrawn from service in 1974 and sold.

The rival Colonial Navigation Company started in 1930 with two relatively elderly steamships, soon to be joined by an equally elderly third ship, and all three were scrapped in 1950 when two new liners replaced them on the Africa run. The 13,200 ton sister-ships "Patria" and "Imperio" were laid down in John Brown's famous shipyard on the Clyde in 1948. They offered luxurious accommodation at a service speed of 17 knots, and like the rival Line's "Angola" and "Mocambique" were very popular with South Africans. But here again dying trade to the Portugese colonies forced their withdrawal from service in 1973, both vessels going to Taiwanese shipbreakers.

The last passenger liner to be laid down for the Colonial Navigation Company was the Belgian built 23,300 ton "Infante Dom Henrique", which made her maiden voyage in 1961. Like the "Principe Perfeito" a beautiful vessel in every respect, she was withdrawn from service and laid up in 1974, a sad and premature end to a fine ship, and marked the closure of an efficient and comfortable ocean passenger service.

In 1956 a new and final chapter opened in the history of the Union-Castle Line when the Cayzer family, founders of the famous Clan Line, gained control of the company, amalgamating the two Lines into the British and Commonwealth Group.

The change in management of the Union-Castle Line was evident when the new "Pendennis Castle" replaced the veteran "Arundel Castle" in the mail fleet in 1958. Laid down as a repeat "Pretoria Castle" her design was modified while under construction, and she came into service as a very different vessel. She was the last Union-Castle liner built by Harland and Wolff, ending the association dating back to 1892.

The first mail-ship to be built to British and Commonwealth specifications was launched from the Cammell Laird yard at Birkenhead by Her Majesty the Queen Mother in June 1959. The 37,600 ton "Windsor Castle" replaced the "Winchester Castle" and set a new standard in luxury travel on the Cape run when she made her maiden voyage to Table Bay on August 18, 1960.

One year later the last passenger liner ordered by the British and Commonwealth Group left John Brown's yard on Clydebank and joined the Union-Castle fleet, replacing the "Carnarvon Castle". The 32,700 ton "Transvaal Castle" was driven by four steam turbines giving her a maximum speed of 23 knots, and was unique in being the Line's only 'Hotel-Class' ship in the mail service.

In May 1963 the British and Commonwealth Group negotiated a new 11 year mail contract with the South African Government, scheduled to come into force on January 1, 1966, cutting passage time for a single voyage to 11.5 days which meant that replacements for the three pre war mail ships would be necessary. There was one advantage in that the new accelerated service allowed seven ships to maintain it as against eight up to that time.

With a fall-off in passenger traffic already lost to the airlines, tenders were invited for two 13,200 ton cargo ships, capable of a service speed of 23 knots, to be brought into the mail service during 1965 to honour the terms of the new mail contract. The "Southampton Castle" and "Good Hope Castle" were capable of maintaining 26 knots, making them the fastest diesel-powered freighters of the time, Initially they carried no passengers, but in 1967 they were required to include calls at St. Helena and Ascension, accommodation for 12 passengers was provided.

With the two freighters joining the mail fleet the "Athlone Castle" was scrapped in August 1965; and "Stirling Castle" in February 1966; while the "Capetown Castle", which for some eighteen months made 16 day voyages between Southampton and the Cape via Madeira, Ascension, St. Helena and Walvis Bay, was eventually disposed of in September 1967.

During 1965 negotiations had been under way with the South African Marine Corporation, in which the British and Commonwealth Group held 25% shareholding, for Safmarine to acquire two Union-Castle mail-ships, to operate in association with the Union-Castle Line.

On January 12, 1966, at a ceremony at Cape Town Docks, the "Transvaal Castle" was renamed "S.A.Vaal", and thereafter sailed in Safmarine livery. Three weeks later at a similar ceremony the "Pretoria Castle" became the "S.A.Oranje" under the Safmarine house-flag. They were subsequently re-registered in Cape Town but both liners continued to be manned predominantly by Union-Castle Line personnel.

In 1963, in a complete departure from previous policy, the British Commonwealth Group chartered the 20,000 ton liner "Reina del Mar" specifically for ocean cruises. She sailed for the Cape in the familiar Union-Castle livery in December 1964, and for the next ten years proved very popular with South African and British passengers. At the end of 1973 she was purchased and then six months later, after a huge fuel price increase, the company announced that she was no longer viable and would be withdrawn from service and sold in April 1975. At the same time the high cost of oil fuel necessitated a speed reduction on the mail service, lengthening passage time to 12.5 days, while passenger traffic steadily transferred to the new jet airliners. The "Edinburgh Castle" and

"S.A.Oranje" were first to be withdrawn, the "S.A.Oranje" sailing to the shipbreakers on October 6, 1975 and the "Edinburgh Castle" in May the following year. Then on July 6, 1976 the "Pendennis Castle" was sold to the Ocean Queen Navigation Corporation, and sailed to Hong Kong allegedly for conversion to a cruise liner but in fact to four years idleness prior to demolition.

The only passenger mail-ships then remaining in the Cape trade were Union-Castle's "Windsor Castle" and Safmarine's "S.A.Vaal", with the two fast 12 passenger freighters "Southampton Castle" and "Good Hope Castle" making calls at St. Helena and Ascension. But for them as well the writing was on the wall. On September 15, 1977 the "Windsor Castle" docked at Southampton for the last time. She was sold to Greek interests and sailed for Piraeus as the "Margareta L" on October 3, while the "S.A.Vaal" on her final arrival at Southampton on October 10, was sold for conversion to a cruise liner based in the United States.

The last sailing on the mail run was undertaken by the "Southampton Castle" exactly 120 years and one day from the departure of the Union steamship "Dane" in 1857, and on her arrival back in her home port on October 24, 1977 the United South Africa mail service had ended.

With the departure of all the passenger ships serving South Africa, a way of life unique to sea travel disappeared. Briefly hopes were raised of a resumption in passenger travel to the United Kingdom when Safmarine purchased the 18,834 ton West German cruise liner "Astor". Well-suited for leisurely voyages, the sustained high speed passage between the Cape and Great Britain overtaxed the "Astor's" six-cylinder diesel engines, and breakdowns were frequent. Three years later she was sold to East German interests, while in 1987 a second "Astor" of similar design, but measuring 20,000 tons was purchased from the West German shipyard that had built her predecessor.

The new liner was registered in Mauritius and sailed under the Mauritian flag, while her cabin and catering staff were Mauritians. Safmarine opened offices in Dorset in England under a different name, to avoid any South African connection with the new liner, but for some reason or another the venture failed. By 1989 the second "Astor" had been sold to the Russians and once again South Africans yearning for the days of ocean travel were disappointed.

With the departure of the "Southampton Castle" and "Good Hope Castle" there were no longer any ships to provide the vital link between the islands of St. Helena and Ascension and the United Kingdom, and the Foreign and Commonwealth office in London called for tenders to provide this service.

With long established shipping Lines, having vast experience of the Cape passenger trade, voluntarily relinquishing passenger services to South Africa, it took a great deal of courage to 'swim against the tide'. But before the end of 1977 it was announced in London that a hitherto little known concern, Curnow Shipping Ltd., with its head office in Cornwall, would institute a regular service to the islands.

And because so many 'Saints' had relatives and long established ties with South Africa, as well as for the freight and passenger potential, the new service would continue through to Cape Town, providing a limited number of passengers the opportunity of once again travelling between Britain and the Cape by sea.

III   CURNOWS OF CORNWALL

Of all the unlikely places in the British Isles in which to find a flourishing shipping company the sleepy fishing harbour of Porthleven in Cornwall must be hard to beat! Nonetheless Porthleven is where Andrew Bell located the head office of Curnow Shipping Limited, initially in a tiny cottage at Number 2, Church Row, and subsequently in The Shipyard, still actively engaged in the repair and maintenance of fishing and other small craft.

The saga of Curnow Shipping is so unusual as to confound any present day economist. One can imagine oneself back in the 16th Century, when the little ships crept out of the small ports into the vast oceans of the world. It is a reincarnation of the merchant venturers, elbowing the company accountants aside.

Himself a fourth generation Cornishman, Andrew Bell was actually born in Sydney, New South Wales, the son of a wool merchant, in 1934. With a deep seated love for the sea at the age of sixteen he became apprenticed to Alfred Holt and Company of Liverpool and served his time with their Blue Funnel Line.

Having acquired his Second Mate's ticket and the rank of Third Officer Andrew Bell decided in 1958 to further his career by becoming a Management Trainee with Elder Dempster Lines also of Liverpool, a company that was to become an associate of Alfred Holt and Company in 1965.

Andrew admits that he went to sea with the ambition of getting into trade. He wanted the pure joy of positioning a ship into a chunk of trade that nobody else had thought of, and this philosophy has made a major contribution to the success of the company he was eventually to found. He had adopted an unusual approach, for the bright young executives in British shipping tend to follow the advice of W.S.Gilbert 'to stick close to their desks and never go to sea!'

For the next fifteen years Andrew acquired knowledge and experience of ship management in every respect, both in the United Kingdom and West Africa with Elder Dempster.

In 1965 Holts took over Elder Dempster, forming with Blue Funnel the second largest British fleet after P & O. The takeover discouraged Andrew who considered that the size of the new concern meant that all the folksy individualism of the second XI of British shipping was swept away. The products of the Harvard School of Business Management, in his opinion, ate up everything on the premise 'the bigger the better'. "The rat race was so intensified" he said, "that there seemed to be more fun in creating my own mouse race!"

But the time was not yet ripe, and in 1965 and 1966 Andrew was back in West Africa as the company's Freight representative at Lagos. In 1967

Veryan, Richard, Prue and Andrew Bell (with Rory)

(A. M. B. Bell)

he returned to Merseyside in the Cargo Care department, and also got married. His wife Prue was born in Lancashire, but had lived in Cornwall for some years before her marriage. They are a happy devoted couple with two children and a gregarious Staffordshire Bull Terrier named Rory. Their daughter Veryan is a secretary, fluent in both French and Spanish, while their son Richard is a student at Bristol Polytechnic.

The year after his marriage to Prue, Andrew was back in West Africa as Operations Manager at Apapa, before further promotion and responsibilities there and in Liverpool. His achievements while with Elder Dempster included the introduction in 1970 of the first Ro-Ro (roll on/roll off) freight service between the United Kingdom and Nigeria, and in the previous year passenger cruises out of Lagos. He was also involved in the operations for the fortnightly mail service between Liverpool and West African ports, employing the mail-ships "Aureol", "Apapa" and "Accra", passenger vessels eventually replaced by cargo-liners.

From the start of his seagoing career Andrew Bell planned for the day he could go into the shipping business on his own account, and every penny he could save was set aside to provide the capital necessary to achieve his ambition.

He saw his opportunity with the rounds of price increases made by the Organization of Petroleum-Exporting Countries (Opec), when oil producing countries, Nigeria included, began a spending spree, In 1974 he was ready to take the plunge, and resigning from Elder Dempster Lines he founded Curnow Shipping on a shoestring. With his Nigerian contacts and a source of supply from British companies, Andrew began to carry building materials to Nigeria in chartered ships. Others had climbed onto the same bandwagon, and at one time 200 ships carrying concrete were waiting in a bizarre log-jam outside the port of Lagos. By using small vessels Andrew avoided the delays and the business flourished.

In 1976 Curnow Shipping Limited was registered with a capital of 40,000 £1 shares, with Andrew as its Founder and Managing Director. There are 13 shareholders, Andrew and his Co-Director and right-hand man Simon Sugrue holding a third each, with the remaining third divided between eleven senior staff, both shore-based and sea-going, thereby enabling his close colleagues to hold a personal stake in the company's future.

Andrew's great-grandfather had been a successful businessman in the north of England, but subsequently for the sake of his wife's deteriorating health, moved in the 1890s to the clean, fresh air that Cornwall provided, and settled in the tiny fishing village of Porthleven.

With a deep-seated affection for the Cornish village that had been the home of his ancestors for three generations, it was natural for Andrew to choose Porthleven in which to establish his new enterprise, and the office of Curnow Shipping Ltd was duly installed in a small 17th Century cottage, situated on a promontory overlooking Mounts Bay. The name, incidentally, derives from the ancient Cornish nomenclature for Cornwall, Kernow, a fitting name for a Cornish based company, anglicised to Curnow.

When in 1981 the Department of the Environment forced Andrew to move his company's modest office from Number 2 Church Row overlooking the Bay, Curnow Shipping Ltd was re-established in equally unpretentious premises just down the road, in the former offices of a boat building concern in what is still called The Shipyard, situated on the waterfront, for Porthleven, which lies on the eastern shoreline of Mounts Bay, is still very much an active fishing harbour.

Despite his deep involvement with Curnow Shipping, Andrew still finds time for extra-mural activities. As an officer in the Royal Naval Reserve he did his National Service with the Royal Australian Navy in 1957 and 1958, and is an active member of the Naval Control of Shipping with the rank of Lieutenant-Commander RNR. He has been awarded the Reserve Decoration with Clasp, and holds Royal Naval Reserve Command qualification.

Naval activities are by no means Andrew's only outside interest, for he serves his local community with the same intensity and enthusiasm that he displays in his business life. He is Chairman of the Cornwall Committee of the Prince's Trust; is Chairman of the Board of Governors of the Duchy Grammar School, Tregye; was Chairman of the Porthleven (Business) Association from 1985 to 1988; is a Member of the Penwith District Council Ports and Pilotage Advisory Committee; and was Chairman of the Trinity House Pilotage sub Commissioners for Penzance with Newlyn, and St. Ives with Hayle from 1978 to 1988. He is also a Fellow of the Institute of Directors, an Associate of the Nautical Institute, and co-author of a book "The Pirrie Kylsant Motorships, 1915–1932".

Curnow Shipping's special strength lies in Ship Management, wherein all services are provided to an owner, including manning; maintenance; insurance; commercial; bunkering etc.. Other facets of their operations include acting as Port Agents in Falmouth for Sealink, Sea Containers and a number of smaller concerns; while having the ability to provide prompt and efficient service with special shipping requirements; and acting as Shipbrokers.

Covering such a broad spectrum of the shipping trade obviously requires an experienced team, and Andrew leads a strong force of experts headed by genial Simon Sugrue. Before joining the company in 1976, Simon was a Master Mariner with extensive command experience. Born in 1940 he went to sea at the age of sixteen with Shell Tankers, and from 1957 to 1964 served from Apprentice to Chief Officer. He then joined the Commonwealth Lighthouse Service in Australia in 1964, and served them until 1968 as Chief Officer, when he became a partner in a company of Marine Surveyors and Consultants, A.M.Leckie and Associates. For the next three years Simon gained valuable experience in cargo survey work, as Lloyds surveyor; and in undertaking non-exclusive American Bureau of Shipping survey work in Fremantle and North Western Australia; at the same time doing Relief Command on off-shore supply and drilling vessels, which from 1972 to 1975 he commanded in Australian waters and as far afield as Korea, Taiwan, Cambodia, Indonesia, Papua and Singapore.

Married in 1964, Simon and his wife are happily settled in Cornwall where their only son practises as a Doctor. They also have three daughters, the eldest of whom at the time of writing was serving as Assistant Catering Purser in the cargo-passenger vessel "Avalon"; while the second works on the Scilly Isles; and the youngest is studying at Manchester University.

Simon is a member of the Honourable Company of Master Mariners; of the Nautical Institute; a Fellow of the Institute of Directors; and past Honorary Secretary of the Royal National Lifeboat Institution's Lizard Lifeboat, an organisation in which he continues to take a keen interest. His winter recreation is skiing, while in summer he sails a racing Cornish Crabber.

At Curnow Shipping Ltd. Simon Sugrue is responsible for Company Development. A good example of what this entails is the recent launch of a new shipping service in the Indian Ocean employing the Curnow managed motorship "Avalon", on behalf of Sea Safaris (Malta) Ltd. This necessitated his presence in Durban for some three months, while the vessel underwent an extensive refit before commencing her new scheduled service, carrying passengers and cargo between Durban and Mombasa, by way of Madagascar and the Comores Islands.

The third member of Curnow Shipping's management team is their Technical Director David Brock, who joined the company as Technical Manager in July 1979 and was appointed to the Board on December 1, 1987. A Chartered Engineer and Fellow of the Institute of Marine Engineers, David was trained by the B.P. Tanker Company under the Alternative Training Scheme which started in 1958.

David sailed in both steam, and diesel-oil tankers in positions ranging from Junior to Chief Engineer, gaining a First Class Extra (Combined) Certificate of Competence in 1971. He also gained experience with Lloyd's Register, as well as a Very Large Crude Carrier (VLCC); and subsequently sailed as Chief Engineer, gaining further experience in VLCCs and Product tankers.

Since joining Curnow Shipping David Brock has been responsible for a wide variety of vessels, including coastal cargo ships, a foreign-going freighter, a cargo-passenger ship, a small Products tanker, and a Ro-Ro ferry.

The fourth member of the Board is Jonathan Challacombe, who came ashore in 1979 to take a degree course in Maritime Studies at Plymouth, and who was appointed a Director of the company on July 10, 1981. A former Chief Officer with the Line, Jonathan holds a Class Two Certificate of Competence (Deck) as well as a Royal Yachting Association Offshore Certificate. He is also a guest lecturer at Plymouth Polytechnic, as well as for professional business groups both in the United Kingdom and New Zealand, and has had Papers published in Nautical Publications dealing with the subject of Ship Management.

He was appointed a Falmouth Harbour Commissioner on January 1, 1991 and is an active member of the General Council of the British Shipping Training Committee for the revalidation of the Deck Cadet System. It is therefore not surprising that Jonathan Challcombe should be a Lieutenant-Commander (Sea Cadet Corps) in the Royal Naval Reserve and Commanding Officer of the Training Ship "Robert Hichens", the Sea Cadet unit that serves Falmouth and Penryn.

Despite his many other committments he still finds the time to be a member of the Penryn Police Consultative Committee, and to serve as a nominated Lay Visitor appointed by the West Cornwall Police Sub-division, two areas in which his wealth of experience in Industrial Relations must be invaluable.

At Curnow Shipping Jonathan Challcombe is responsible pre-dominantly for Operations, in addition to being Training Manager and Ship's Husband. This latter designation dates back to the days of sail, and referred to the person formerly carried in a merchant ship to transact ship's business and to purchase stores. In earlier times the Ship's Husband was the Boatswain who was also in charge of the crew, and of the fabric of the ship, and in general terms the Ship's Husband has the same responsibilities today.

Completing the management team is Christopher Gardner, who joined the company as Finance Manager and Company Secretary in May 1988, with a background that must surely be unique in business circles. Obtaining a scholarship with the united Kingdom Atomic Energy Authority, Chris studied Physics at Manchester University from 1964 to 1967, gaining his BSc with Honours.

He thereupon joined the Royal Navy, and after training at the Royal Naval Colleges at Dartmouth and at Greenwich, served as a Lieutenant in a number of appointments. After specialising in Meteorology and Oceanography he was promoted to Lieutenant-Commander, and gained extensive experience over a ten-year period in both sea-going and shore appointments, including those of Senior Meteorologist in HMS "Daedalus", HMS "Seahawk" and the Flying Training School at RNAS Culdrose, at Helston in Cornwall.

On completion of the Royal Navy's Medium Career Commission, and after studying Accountancy in his off-duty periods, Chris retired from the Service in the rank of Lieutenant-Commander and was articled to Spicer and Oppenheim, Chartered Accountants in London. He transferred in 1985 to become Management Accountant at Carnon Tin Mines Ltd. for three years, before joining Curnow Shipping Ltd in his current capacity.

By the end of 1976 the volume of trade to Nigeria had grown significantly, justifying the formation of a separate company. To this end Curnow Shipping Ltd, in association with Allpalm, the company whose building materials their chartered vessels were carrying, and with shipowner Michael Bustard, registered Commonwealth Lines on January 4, 1977, with Curnow Shipping holding 15% of the share capital and Simon Sugrue as its Managing Director. Curnow's role was to act as Shipbrokers, employing two small Danish freighters and the 1,680 ton "Pentire" owned by Michael Bustard. The "Pentire" had been acquired from a South African concern, Unicorn Shipping Line, and was manned by Curnow Shipping personnel.

For four years Commonwealth Lines carried building materials to Nigeria before a fall in demand brought this joint venture to an end in 1981, when the company was liquidated.

Meanwhile, in 1975 Andrew Bell became aware of a development that was to change the whole nature of his company, namely the impending containerisation of the Cape route. Realising that such a vast programme would require huge investment, Andrew concluded that there were bound to be areas which would not be covered. In the same year a British firm of Accountants, Peat Marwick Mitchell, undertook an investigation commissioned in the light of the stated intention of the Union-Castle Line to withdraw their mail-ships on the Cape run by the end of October 1977, and to cease their regular calls at St. Helena and Ascension. How were the two islands to be catered for thereafter?

Andrew Bell realised immediately that here was an area which would not be covered under the proposed containerisation programme, and began an investigation of his own. Having established that the shipping trade to St. Helena and Ascension was controlled by the Foreign and Commonwealth Office of the British Government, Andrew dug out what information there was concerning discharge facilities, cargo handling and steverdoring at Jamestown and Georgetown, to ascertain what type of vessel would be best suited for the purpose.

He then contacted Peat Marwick Mitchell, asking for whatever information they could let him have. In his own words "they reacted with total British gentlemanliness, and instead of saying 'what is this half-pint company?' sent me all the information I had requested".

But as is so often the case when dealing with Government departments, the consultant's report vanished into the Foreign Office and nothing more was heard of the project for the next 18 months, but at Curnow Shipping a file had been opened and was kept up-to-date, albeit the volume of other business occupying the Management's attention necessitated the file being worked on over weekends only.

At stake was a contract to provide a ship to carry cargo and passengers to the two islands on a scheduled service. But with larger companies concentrating on containerised cargoes such a vessel sailing onto Cape

Town would also provide the only passenger service by sea once the mail-ships had been withdrawn.

"In terms of cash and credibility" reflected Andrew Bell, "It was our real break into the big time. We were moving from our specialised base of ferrying building materials into our own mini-liner trade." Then confident that once tenders were called for, the company with the right vessel readily available at the right price would clinch the contract, Curnow Shipping commenced a world-wide search for a suitable cargo-passenger ship.

The ship in question was located in Vancouver. Owned by a Dutch concern she had been engaged on what was termed 'the grocery run ' up to the fjords of British Columbia between Vancouver and Anchorage, Alaska, taking cargo and passengers. But when the Canadian Government had withdrawn a subsidy paid to the line, the ship had been taken out of service and was laid up pending disposal.

Her design was such that the vessel's stern was that of a small passenger liner, while the rest of her was fitted out for handling cargo. And with her ability to accommodate up to 100 passengers she was ideal for the purpose.

By early 1977 the Foreign Office realised the urgency of finding a replacement for the Union-Castle Line. Many companies were approached, and when those interested withdrew the Government started to play off the remainder by calling for tenders, which ploy occupied seven vital months. During this period of negotiation Curnow Shipping made no fewer than nine separate presentations, only to find on each occasion that the "ground rules had been changed", as Andrew Bell put it!

Meanwhile much activity was taking place at Curnow Shipping. They had the ship, but if the contract came their way they lacked the finance to acquire it. In March that year Simon Sugrue went up to London to call on a Merchant Bank, United International, to seek the necessary financial backing. The outcome was an undertaking by United International that provided Curnow Shipping Limited was awarded the contract, the bank was prepared to make the company a loan of £1 million. And as Simon reports the negotiations took just 12 minutes for the necessary guarantee to be forthcoming! Subseqeuntly United International Bank admitted to Simon that the initial interview had taken only 12 minutes because they did not believe that Curnow Shipping could get the contract. They were in fact very surprised when Curnow Shipping came back to them with the contract and requested the money!

Curnow has also agreed a price for the ship in Vancouver, once again subject to the contract going their way. Eventually it was to cost them £940,000, a bargain in the circumstances. Andrew Bell and a team of experts had already examined the vessel very thoroughly, and were happy with its overall condition. Now it was the turn of the Foreign Office to satisfy themselves that the ship could carry out the service. Officials of the Department of transport flew to Vancouver for this purpose, and once their approval had been voiced Curnow Shipping Limited was awarded the contract.

The Vessel was of 3,150 tons, and had been launched in 1963 as the "Northland Prince", but before sailing from Vancouver the United Kingdom via the Panama Canal on November 5, 1977, she was renamed "St. Helena".

The contract required Curnow to form a separate company to operate the vessel, and the St. Helena Shipping Company was accordingly registered as a wholly owned subsidiary.

The United International Bank's liability was limited to their loan of £1 million, with the ownership of the ship passing to them as security. the British Treasury were to pay the cost of converting the "St. Helena" for her new role on behalf of the Government of St. Helena, who in turn chartered the ship from the United International Bank and appointed the St. Helena Shipping Company to manage, operate and man the vessel for a ten year period. This agreement in fact expired in 1988, but was extended year by year until the new RMS "St. Helena" came into service on October 26, 1990.

The St. Helena Shipping Company was formally registered on October 12 1977, but before the "St. Helena" went to Vosper Ship Repairers for conversion she sailed for the Islands on a proving voyage on December 12, 1977, loaded with general cargo, including rice, second-hand cars and lavatory paper, as well as a small party of St. Helenans and Government representatives!

After these initial visits to Ascension and St. Helena, the "St. Helena" docked at Table Bay for the first time on January 8, 1978. She was not to be seen at the Cape again for almost twelve months, only returning to South African waters on her third official round voyage on December 29, 1978.

The St. Helenans heard the welcome news that their isolation from the outside world would soon be over in an announcement contained in the 'St. Helena News Review' dated September 2, 1977. It read as follows:-

"Royal Mail Vessel "St. Helena". The following is a summary of the main points concerning the new shipping service for St. Helena, the full text of which was broadcast by the Hon. R.G. Buckley from the Government Radio Station on Wednesday and Thursday this week . . . It has now been agreed with a Cornish firm, Curnow Shipping Ltd., to set up a new and separate company which will be named the St. Helena Shipping Company Ltd. This company will negotiate the purchase and conversion of the vessel "Northland Prince" which, after consultation with the St. Helenan Government, has now been renamed RMV "St. Helena". The St. Helenan Government will enter into a Management Agreement with the St. Helena Shipping Company under which the company will undertake the management required in providing a continuous scheduled service to convey cargo and passengers to St. Helena and Ascension, and other commercial traffic, to destinations on the agreed route . . .

The vessel will be painted green below water, white hull above waterline, white accommodation and masts with grey derricks. Arrangements are in hand with the hope of registering the vessel in St Helena together with registering the new company here. The ship will fly the St. Helena house-flag, which is the sign of the old East India Company's sea-lion on a green background. The funnel will also bear this sign on both sides.

It is planned for the vessel to sail from Vancouver about September 1, and to arrive in the United Kingdom about September 30, where the conversion work, final surveys etc., will be carried out. It is hoped that the vessel will be ready to sail from the United Kingdom by the first week in December for her first voyage . . .

The run between Avonmouth and Las Palmas (later Tenerife) will be 5 days; between Las Palmas and Ascenion 6 days; Ascension to St. Helena 2 days; and St. St. Helena to Cape Town 5 days. With a stop of about 2 days each at Ascension and St. Helena to discharge cargo, the round trip will be in about 48 days.

This vessel, being classed as a passenger ship will not be able to carry petrol for the Island. She will carry out diesel fuel and paraffin supplies, but petrol presents another problem . . .

It is hoped to crew the RMV "St. Helena" with a St. Helenan crew, which will consist of a Bosun; 7 Deckhands; 3 Greasers; Chief Cook; Second Cook; and 10 Catering Staff. Our new service will be very much a trial and error operation in the beginning, and there will be many problems with the service for the first year or so, but once everybody, including the new managers, new agencies in the ports of call, and the users get the feel of the service it is hoped that things will run smoothly".

The news of the impending new service between the United Kingdom and Cape Town reached South Africa when the following news items appeared on November 1, 1977 in the "Pretoria News".

Mr. Andrew Bell, head of a Cornish cargo firm which is to manage a new shipping service between Britain and Cape Town by way of St. Helena and Ascension, believes there is a great scope for passengers on the service.

'We very much hope that we can follow in the wake of Union-Castle' he said. 'We are very much encouraged by the fact that in 1976 Safmarine and Union-Castle carried just under 26,000 passengers between the United Kingdom and South Africa.

If we fill every berth that we have got to spare over the Island's need, we shall be after just over 3% of the passengers who travelled by sea last year between the United Kingdom and South Africa.' He said he was 'frankly staggered' that Union-Castle and Safmarine had given away, or abdicated a passenger trade of that size.

'I know it is very seasonal . . . but that's one hell of a trade to give away!'

Mr. Bell is Managing Director of Curnow Shipping of Porthleven, Cornwall, which will manage and participate in the new company St. Helena Shipping.

The company recently paid R1.6 million for the "Northland Prince", a 3,150 ton vessel which was used to operate between Vancouver and Alaska. Renamed the "St. Helena" it will operate the new service six times a year from the port of Avonmouth."

In the announcement of the new shipping service contained in the 'St. Helena News Review' it was stressed that as a passenger ship the RMS St. Helena" would not be able to carry the Island's petrol supplies. To meet this requirement Curnow Shipping Ltd. in November 1981 acquired on behalf of the St. Helena Shipping Company a 565 deadweight tonnage tanker.

This small tanker "Cherrybobs", launched as the "Esso Dover", was renamed "Bosun Bird", and for the next seven years supplied the Island's needs. The "Bosun Bird" was disposed of in 1989 when the St. Helenan Government exercised its prerogative to do its own importation of petrol and other fuels.

From 1982 to 1985 Curnow Shipping manned and operated a small coaster "St. Anne of Alderney" between Plymouth and Alderney, in addition to being part owners of the vessel. Also during 1982 and 1983 the company manned and operated a small freighter "Cedra Sun" which had been in Lisbon, outward bound from Hamburg to Asunsion in Paraguay, when she came under Curnow Shipping Management. Asunsion lies some 700 miles up the River Plate, and on her arrival there the "Cedra Sun" was the first British ship to call at the port for 20 years.

On departing Ascunsion homeward bound the "Cedra Sun" proceeded down the River Plate, an Argentine Pilot replacing the Paraguayan one when the vessel reached Argentine waters. Unfortunately the Falkland War had just started and the Argentine Pilot was obliged to report the presence in Argentine waters of the British Ship. Fortunately for the the "Cedra Sun" and her crew the Argentine authorities failed to get their act together, and her Master, Captain Mike Underwood, was able to ring emergency full ahead and to seek the sanctuary of Uruguayan waters!

For six years, from 1980 to 1986, Curnow Shipping Ltd. managed the 9,387 ton Ro-Ro liner "Rangatira", which they also manned in conjunction with the Blue Star Line. During this period the "Rangatira" took part in the Falklands campaign, as did the RMS "St. Helena"; it was also necessary from time to time to charter on behalf of the St. Helena Shipping Company, a total of 14 small freighters to cope with the volume of cargo consigned to the two Atlantic Islands.

In 1987 Curnow Shipping Ltd. was appointed Agent for the port of Falmouth for both Sealink Ferries and Sea Containers, in addition to other smaller concerns, responsibilities including the care, maintenance and modifications of 4 laid-up ships. Furthermore during 1987 and 1988 they acted as managers, for a four month period, of Turkish Lines damaged vessel "Benwalid".

A final example of the diversity of their shipping interests is their appointment as Broker and Consultant to the Isles of Scilly, as well as operating on Charter during the winter months of 1987/88, in conjunction with Robert Francis and Associates, the small Danish freighter "Jenka". The "Jenka" was employed in ferrying building materials from Gweek in Cornwall to St. Martins in the Scilly Isles; while subsequent to the "Jenka" Curnow Shipping undertook the cargo building as well as operating the ex-landing craft (cargo) "Puffin Billy".

Not every venture undertaken by Curnow Shipping Ltd. has been successful. There have been two unhappy experiences which proved costly to the company. The first of these involved the 8,665 gross registered ton liner "World Renaissance", which had been built for French interests in 1966, and subsequently sold to Greek owners in 1977, who operated the vessel as a cruise ship.

This was a joint venture in 1983 with a South African travel organization T.F.C. Tours specializing in package tours, and the "World Renaissance" was chartered for five months to carry passengers between South Africa and the United Kingdom.

Unfortunately for both parties the timing proved totally wrong, as without their knowledge Safmarine had acquired the 20,000 ton West German liner "Astor", and was operating in direct competition with them. Furthermore, the "World Renaissance" proved to be completely unsuited for the lengthy voyages and the joint venture cost Curnow Shipping £300,000.

The second misfortune to befall Andrew Bell was another joint venture, on this occasion with a New Zealand operator. A company was formed to operate a ferry service between Wellington on the North Island and Port Lyttleton on the South, with Curnow Shipping winning the manning contract. Vested interests in the form of New Zealand Railways caused this joint venture to go out of business, and the company was liquidated.

Curnow Shipping's most recent undertaking, supervised by Simon Sugrue, was to launch a project by Sea Safaris (Malta) Ltd to operate a four weekly service between Durban and Mombasa, made possible by political changes in South Africa. Fortuitously the delivery of the new RMS "St. Helena", which released her predecessor to embark on some other operation, had come at the right time to take advantage of the revived shipping trade offer. In November 1990, the "St. Helena" (I) was sold to Sea Safaris (Malta) Ltd who realised the potential for cruising in the Indian Ocean. Renamed "Avalon" the vessel sailed for Durban under the Maltese flag to be refurbished prior to fulfilling the new role for which she was so aptly suited.

As the Director responsible for Company Development, Simon Sugrue flew to Durban to supervise the ship's refit, and to get the new project afloat. Initially manned, managed and operated by Curnow Shipping Ltd on behalf of her new owners, the "Avalon" maintained a scheduled four week service between Durban and Mombasa, carrying passengers and freight, with calls at Tulear and Nose Be in Madagascar, and Mayotte and Moroni in the Comores Islands.

Curnow Shipping Ltd is keenly interested in tendering for a new inter-island ferry service between St. Helena and Ascension, which the British Government has been investigating on behalf of the Government of St. Helena; but the prospects of the Treasury financing such a project is, in Andrew Bell's opinion, very doubtful in the immediate future. Should the money be forthcoming, and the planned service a reality, Curnow must, with their proven expertise, have a better than even chance of securing the contract to man and operate such a service.

Were this to happen it would obviate the need for the RMS "St. Helena" to undertake the St. Helena/Ascension/St. Helena shuttle service each voyage, both southbound for the Cape and on her homeward voyage. The saving of the eight days this exercise consumes would allow the St. Helena Shipping Company to increase the present six round voyages each year between Cardiff and Cape Town to seven, bringing increased benefits to both the islanders and operators.

For some years now, Andrew Bell has had his sights firmly fixed on the Pacific, which he believes holds many opportunities for an enterprising shipowner. He has in fact already established an understanding with a Californian exporter, which has led them to jointly registering a company, Pacific Island Navigation Line.

The intention is for Curnow Shipping to manage, operate and man a container-liner service from San Francisco to the mid-Pacific, capable of lifting 400 T E U's (Twenty foot equivalent units) and of accommodating some 200 passengers.

Such a schedule service promises enormous potential, as quite apart from a conveniently available source of Americans to embark on such a round voyage, it is conceivable that in co-operation with an air-charter company, passengers from the United Kingdom could be flown to and from San Francisco for an all-inclusive cruise to the exotic South Sea Islands.

Another instance of Andrew Bell's forward thinking was his acquisition of the defunct Glen Line in March 1989. The only assets that this dormant company had to offer were the company books and records, plus more importantly, its name, still held in the highest regard in British shipping circles.

As far back as 1869 the Glen Line, in association with the Shire Line, was trading with the Far East, and in 1911 it was one of Lord Kylsant's earlier acquisitions when he was in the process of building up his formidable shipping empire. In 1935, following the collapse of the Kylsant Group, Glen Line became closely associated with Alfred Holt & Co, and only ceased trading in the late 1970s. It gave Andrew Bell immense satisfaction to acquire the Glen Line as a wholly owned subsidiary of Curnow Shipping Ltd. In the future he envisages employing luxury catamarans, proudly flying the Glen Line house-flag, for cruising in the Hebrides, where one small luxuriously equipped cruise ship, "Hebridean Princess", has been in service since 1989.

Of 1,420 gross registered tons, the "Hebridean Princess" was launched as the MacBrayne Lines Island Ferry "Columba", but has been redesigned and fitted out with accommodation for just 46 passengers in great comfort. Operating out of Oban, alternating with Kyle of Lochalsh, she has rarely sailed with an empty berth in her three seasons to date, which commence in early April and continue through to the end of October.

With her limited passenger capacity, the "Hebridean Princess" undertakes some 27 cruises annually, varying in length from three nights on board to seven, with one extended sailing lasting a fortnight. In an entire season therefore, the maximum number that the vessel can cater for would be 782 passengers, and to date the majority appear to be drawn from the Highlands itself.

Clearly Andrew Bell's plan has possibilities, and the prospect of sailing The Minchs, with all their scenic attractions, using one or more catamarans specifically designed for cruising, is an alluring prospect, but beyond the scope of this study.

IV   THE FIRST OF THE "SAINTS"

On October 12, 1977 the St. Helena Shipping Company was registered as a wholly owned subsidiary of Curnow Shipping Ltd., to manage, operate and man a suitable vessel under charter to the St. Helenan Government. The vessel acquired for this purpose, the "Northland Prince", had been built by the Burrard Dry Dock Company in 1963 for the Vancouver-Alaskan coastal trade. She was 321 feet long and measured 3,150 gross registered tons. With 135,000 cubic feet of cargo space, berths for 88 passengers, and a service speed of 14 knots provided by a single screw 4,200 brake horse power Stork Werkspoor diesel engine, she was ideal for the Island trade. Renamed "St. Helena" she sailed from Vancouver for the United Kingdom on November 5, 1977 and docked at Avonmouth, which was to become her home port for the next thirteen years. After a single 'proving' voyage to Ascension and St. Helena, the St. Helena returned to the United Kingdom and docked at Southampton, prior to undergoing conversion before entering service.

From the beginning of November 1977, until the refurbished RMS "St. Helena made her maiden scheduled voyage on September 13 the following year, the islands were supplied by chartered ships, including the Greek owned "Semiramis". Originally built for Elder Dempster Lines in 1938, the forty year old veteran was chartered for a single round voyage, with three St. Helena Shipping Company officers on board as supernumaries, the senior Navigation Officer, the Purser, and the Catering Officer. The "Semiramis" carried no cargo, only mail, but could accommodate 100 passengers. Northbound she embarked at Jamestown the St. Helenans who were to join the RMS "St. Helena" as the vessel's Catering staff upon completion of her refit and conversion.

The arrival of the "St. Helena" at Southampton to undergo conversion after her initial 'proving' voyage was recorded in the January 31, 1978 issue of the City's newspaper 'Southern Echo' in the following words:-

"The 3,150 ton passenger-cargo ship "St. Helena" docked at Southampton yesterday after completing a proving voyage in the Cape Town Atlantic Isles Service, formerly maintained by the Union-Castle Line's "Good Hope Castle" and Southampton Castle".
The intention is to use the "St. Helena" in this service, with probably Avonmouth as the U.K. departure port. The Southampton call was arranged because the ship is to entrusted to Vosper Ship Repairers, who will carry out various alterations and overhaul work on board. The "St. Helena", which was delayed on her homeward voyage by bad weather, had a small cargo including mail from islands, five tons of general cargo, empty containers, and a dog" . . .

While work on the ship was in hand, the Southampton 'Southern Echo' published an article in the April 17 issue detailing the extent of the conversion necessary to enable the "St. Helena" to carry out her new role to best advantage

> "Vosper Ship Repairers, a member of British Shipbuilders, are carrying out an interesting overhaul and conversion job aboard the 3,150 ton "St. Helena", which is to provide a link between the UK and the Atlantic Islands and Cape Town.
>
> . . . Apart from overhauls and inspection, cleaning and painting, Vospers are doing conversion work to bring the ship upto international standards for passenger carrying.
>
> This involves improved accommodation for 88 passengers and for the crew; increased oil fuel and water tanks; new radio room and operator's cabin; hospital; surgery and bathroom complex. Various structural alterations are also in progress to improve fire resistance and to meet the latest requirements. Sprinklers and fire extinguisher systems are being extensively modified. Other conversion work included new lifeboats and davits and other life-saving equipment; re-equipping the galley in a new layout; fitting a new laundry and drying room; and installing new water-tight doors. The project is expected to take about 4 months and cost £750,000."

The work in fact took some six months to complete, while the cost escalated to £1.5 million, before the ship was ready to commence her scheduled voyages on the Cape run. But before her official maiden voyage to the Islands there was the formal renaming ceremony at Southampton on August 2, 1978 performed by H.R.H. The Princess Margaret. Following the ceremony Captain Martin Smith and his officers were presented to Her Royal Highness, prior to her lunching with them. It was a proud day for Andrew Bell and his colleagues.

The RMS "St. Helena" left Avonmouth for Ascension and St. Helena, by way of Las Palmas, on September 13, 1978; and on this first voyage, and the following one, did not continue to Cape Town, returning instead from the Islands to her home port. Only on Voyage 3 was her sailing extended to Cape Town, where she docked on her first official arrival on December 29 that year. Proudly flying her Royal Mail pennant—the only vessel undertaking long ocean voyages still to do so—the appearance of the "St. Helena" in Table Bay was the extension of a tradition that had begun 128 years before.

For obvious reasons the comparatively small RMS did not represent a return to the glamour and elegance of the "Castle" lines. Rather she made her own reputation as an excellent seaboat providing good, wholesome meals, accompanied by friendly service of a high standard provided by her St. Helenan stewards and stewardesses.

Initially the RMS "St. Helena" was under command of Captain Martin Smith, one of the very few mariners currently at sea with his Master's ticket in sail. Alternating with Captain Smith was Captain Bob Wyatt, an ex-Union-Castle mailship officer, as were many others serving with the St. Helena Shipping Company.

Devotees of the Castle Liners felt immediately at home on boarding the RMS, for other ex-mail-ship personnel included Purser Colin Dellar; Catering Officer Dave Padmore; Second Steward Ted Durham. 'Dusty' Miller and later Les Farrow; Assistant Pursers Jean Bonner and Angela Read; Chef Paul King; the Bosun Benjamin Jones; Chief Engineer Bryan Gillott; and last but by no means least, Radio Officer Bob Wilson, a Fellow of the Royal Society whose off-duty hobby is the creation of model ships, built precisely to scale and in minute detail.

Accommodation in the "St. Helena" was straight forward but spacious for a vessel of her size. Cabins for the 76 passengers borne were located aft in the Bridge structure on two decks, all with either a porthole or window, and all with private facilities consisting of a shower, toilet and wash basin.

There were two lounges, one forward overlooking the bow, while the other known as the Stern Gallery was located aft, with large windows giving a panoramic view over the ship's wake. The forward lounge, which stretched the full width of the vessel, housed a small but well stocked bar while a small library was located in the Stern Gallery.

The Ship's Office was located adjoining the forward lounge, while the dining saloon, small shop, and do-It-yourself laundry and drying room were one deck down. Deck space was limited, but there was a sun-deck abaft the funnel, and a small portable swimming pool was housed on the foredeck.

The "St. Helena" was no cruise liner. She was a practical cargo-passenger vessel plying her ocean trade in the best traditions of the British Merchantile Marine. The luxury of the old-time liner may have been missing, but the friendly atmosphere that prevailed throughout the ship assured the travelling public of a warm welcome on board, adding to the pleasure of a relaxing ocean voyage that might take up to 24 days to complete.

That the RMS, as the ship was affectionately known, had, on her first official voyage south, immediately established for herself the enviable reputation of being a 'happy ship', is borne out by the following extract from a letter to Andrew Bell from Bert Howe, Chief Executive of Solomon & Co. (St. Helena) Ltd., of Jamestown, the main Government trading company, and inter alia the local agents for the St. Helena Shipping Company, which read as follows:-

"Usual scramble on whilst we unload, so little time for chit chat, but I know you will be pleased to read that passengers (in the RMS "St.

Helena") of all shapes and sizes praises the ship, the food, the cheerful atmosphere, and the attention and entertainment they received".

Certainly there was never a dull moment on board the RMS. The Purser and his assistants, with a wealth of experience in entertaining passengers on a long voyage, saw to that. Apart from various sporting activities during the daylight hours, no evening passed without some form of entertainment, be it Bingo, a Quiz contest, Frog racing, a Whist night, or a Movie show. The three highlights of the voyage were undoubtedly the Fancy Dress night; Bob (Windjammer) Wilson's slide presentations; and definitely top of the pops, the Ship's Concert provided by the ship's officers!

But for those passengers seeking their own company for a quiet evening with a good book, there was always one peaceful spot were this could be achieved. There was plenty of entertainment but no regimentation!

The first official through voyage the RMS made, sailing from Avonmouth on December 6, 1978, was to be a testing one indeed, as this extract from the company's records reveals. Bound for Las Palmas as her first port of call, Captain Martin Smith, was well aware of severe gale warnings in the Bay of Biscay and to westwards of it.

With 61 passengers embarked, including the well-known author Commander Anthony Trew DSC., RNVR, 46 crew members and 436 tons of cargo, the 3,150 gross registered ton vessel steamed at slow speed in the lee of the Cornish peninsula towards Lands End, waiting for the gale force winds to abate.

The following morning Captain Smith anchored his command in St. Ives Bay, joining 14 other ships awaiting relative calm before proceeding south. By noon December 8 the "St. Helena" was buffeting her way into confused rough seas, with a moderate swell and a Force 5 wind. Nothing out of the ordinary for an ocean going vessel, even of "St. Helena's" displacement. The Bay crossing was a lively one under clear skies, but following Divine Service that Sunday morning the barometer began a steady fall.

By 23.00 that night it had fallen an incredible 21 millibars in just eight hours, and as the glass fell so did the wind and the sea rise. Some four hours earlier the ship was hove-to, and by 21.00 the wind was a sustained Force 10, or 55 miles an hour, gusting up to Force 12 by midnight.

First light on the Monday morning revealed those mountainous seas all seafarers dread. Estimated at 60 feet from trough to crest they literally topped the foremast and dwarfed the ship as they raced relentlessly by. With engine revolutions for 7 knots the "St. Helena" was remorselessly driven astern at a rate of 3 knots, with seas breaking over the fo'c'sle and foredeck, and spray lashing the Bridge structure.

By 15.00 the worst was past, the wind having dropped to Force 7, and a course could be laid to the Canary Islands. On the ship's arrival in Las Palmas, her scheduled stay of eight hours to take on fuel and water was

RMS WINDSOR CASTLE saluting RMMV GOOD HOPE CASTLE as she sails on the final Union-Castle passenger and mail sailing, August 1977

(A. S. Mallett)

RMS ST HELENA I at sea

(Curnow Shipping)

Lounge, RMS ST HELENA I

(P. C. Kohler)

Dining Saloon, RMS ST HELENA I

(P. C. Kohler)

(P. C. Kohler)

Bridge, RMS ST HELENA I

79

(P. C. Kohler)

Stern Gallery, RMS ST HELENA I

RMS CENTAUR discharging at Jamestown, April 1983

(P. C. Kohler)

Lido Deck, RMS CENTAUR

(P. C. Kohler)

Sports Deck, RMS CENTAUR

(P. C. Kohler)

RMS ST HELENA ISLAND viewed from RMS ST HELENA II,
Cardiff, October 1990   (A. S. Mallett)

RMS ST HELENA II preparing for her maiden voyage at Cardiff, 1990, with ST HELENA ISLAND astern

(A. S. Mallett)

Sun Lounge, RMS ST HELENA II

(Curnow Shipping)

Cabin B36, RMS ST HELENA II   (Curnow Shipping)

Dining Saloon, RMS ST HELENA II   (Curnow Shipping)

Bridge, RMS ST HELENA II   (A. S. Mallett)

RMS ST HELENA II showing mast design and Royal Mail Pennant,
October 1990   (A. S. Mallett)

RMS ST HELENA II Seahorse motif   (A. S. Mallett)

RMS ST HELENA II

(Curnow Shipping)

extended to twenty-six hours to repair the storm damage. But what minor damage had been incurred, and the loss of three days on her sailing schedule, were indeed a blessing when it is appreciated that in the "storm of storms", as Captain Smith described the ship's ordeal, "a tempest the likes of which none of us will see again", seven vessels foundered.

That the "St. Helena" came through this testing challenge with flying colours was the laconic comment made to the author by Commander Trew following his arrival in Cape Town. A veteran of Russian convoys during the Second World War, he was an experienced seaman. "She's a good seaboat" he said.

From her departure on September 13, 1978 on her maiden voyage south until May 12, 1982, the "St. Helena" maintained her scheduled voyages between Avonmouth, Ascension, St. Helena and Cape Town. Once each year in December a call at Tristan da Cunha was included, governed as the Island was from St. Helena but on May 12, 1982 the "St. Helena" went to war.

When Great Britain commenced operations to recover the Falklands from Argentina the Ministry of Defence requisitioned the RMS for war service. After a hasty refit at Portsmouth, including the mounting of a helicopter landing pad above the Stern Gallery, "St. Helena" became the mother ship to the Fleet minesweepers HM Ships "Brecon" and "Ledbury". After embarking her helicopter and the naval party drafted to serve in the ship, the "St. Helena" left Portland under the command of Captain Martin Smith and a volunteer crew and steamed southwards, where for the next four months she was stationed at both South Georgia and Port Stanley.

When the conflict was over the "St. Helena" returned, to Rosyth and then Portsmouth at the end of September 1982 for her annual refit. The mail-ship was however retained by the Ministry of Defence on indefinite time charter, to continue her role as mother ship to those minesweepers retained in the Falklands to free the waters of Argentine mines. She was to remain under Admiralty orders for the next eight months. During the twelve month period that the "St. Helena" was on charter to the Ministry of Defence she steamed 68,000 miles. Apart from her duty as mother ship to the Fleet minesweepers, she carried almost 1,000 passengers during her time in the South Atlantic, ferrying personnel and supplies between Ascension and Port Stanley once the minefields had been cleared and the minesweepers had returned to the United Kingdom.

When the RMS was requisitioned for war duties Curnow Shipping Ltd., as a stop gap measure, substituted the 522 dead weight ton "Aragonite" to maintain a freight service to the South Atlantic Islands and Cape Town, until a suitable ship could be chartered. By November 1982 Curnow had found such a vessel, and the 7,989 ton "Centaur" owned by the Straits Steamship Company, a subsidiary of the Blue Funnel Line, was chartered for a six month period. When the "St. Helena" was retained by the

Captain Martin Smith and Radio Officer Bob Wilson

(Bob Wilson)

Ministry of Defence on indefinite time charter after the conflict in the Falklands had ended, the "Centaur" charter was extended, and she was retained by Curnow Shipping until November 1983, when she was returned to her owners.

The passages that follow are extracts from the Daily Orders issued on board the "St. Helena" during the vessel's initial four months of duty, during the period immediately after the Falkland's War, while under charter to the Ministry of Defence. By May 29, 1982 the ship had completed her refit, brief as it had been, at Portsmouth and was in all respects ready to proceed south to the war zone.

"May 31, 1982: Daily harbour routine, continue storing ship.
Test RAS gear, inclination trial, return Merchant Navy bedding to ship's laundry.
Now that storing is complete the object is to clean up the ship for sea. Stubbing out of cigarettes on deck and piling up of gash in alleyways is to cease forthwith!
Radio. When the ship sails there will be radio silence for private communication".
"June 1, 1982: Daily harbour routine.
Service personnel will not under any circumstances enter cabins or recreation areas of civilian crew.
Service personnel will not entertain in their sleeping accommodation. All entertainment for junior ratings will take place in the Stern Gallery. Wherever possible the Merchant Navy crew will be controlled by the Ship's Officers, and the Royal Navy party by Service Officers or Senior Rates. Any order given by a Merchant Navy Officer is to be considered that of a Senior Naval Officer. Disciplinary action will immediately follow any insubordination!
DON'T TELL THE PRESS ANYTHING.
All rumour mongers requested to shut up as from now!"
"June 2, 1982: Daily harbour routine.
Flight deck operations will take place today.
. . . All members of the ship's company to have:-
S6 Respirator and spare canister.
Anti-flash gear.
Steel helmets and flak jackets for personnel manning exposed positions.
Life Jacket.
Survival suit.
Mug.
Ear plugs.
Geneva Convention I.D. Card.
IF YOU HAVEN'T GOT IT GET IT BEFORE FRIDAY JUNE 4"

The three ships "St. Helena", HMS "Brecon" and HMS "Ledbury" were scheduled to sail south on June 9, but engine trouble in HMS "Ledbury" delayed their departure for 48 hours.

"June 11, 1982: Commanding Officers RMS "St. Helena", HMS "Brecon", HMS "Ledbury, plus Flight Commander, MO, XO, RS and head of department meet in wardroom 0800.

FOR MERCHANT NAVY CREW. ATTENTION TO INSTRUCTIONS AND ADVICE PIPED OVER THE P.A. SYSTEM IS TOO LAX!

YOU ARE REQUESTED TO LISTEN MORE ATTENTIVELY AND FOLLOWING ANY ADVICE GIVEN. THIS WILL MAKE FOR A BETTER RUN AND EFFECTIVE SHIP!

. . . BE DILIGENT. Censorship is not planned. But do not discuss in letters:-

Operational plans.

Speculation about what might happen.

State of readiness of this or other ships. AS gear, inclination trial, return Merchant Navy bedding to ship's laundry.

Info from Intelligence, or Argentinian plans or capabilities.

Equipment and other defects.

Places visited.

Ships encountered.

Damage received to either your own or enemy units.

If in doubt as to whether to mention it—DON'T!"

"June 12, 1982: Harbour.

Dedication on Flight Deck at 11.00

Secure for sea".

"June 13, 1982: Sea Routine.

RAS trials with "Black Rover".

Prove stern RA with HMS "Brecon".

Rendezvous with HMS "Ledbury" and PROCEED SOUTH".

"June 14, 1982: Sea.

09.15 Flying stations.

13.00 Action stations.

O/C Abandon ship drill.

WELL DONE SHIP'S COMPANY. THANK YOU.

Sea Routine.

Flyex.

Mock casualty transfer (Napoleon dummy).

Zig Zag ex.

Brief Ship's Officers on tactical circuits for RAS, passage formations, low grade codes and BREAD WINDOW.

Darken ship. No navigation lights".

And so, in the company of HM Ships "Brecon" and "Ledbury", the RMS "St. Helena" sailed south to the war zone. Small as she was, with her reinforced stem designed for steaming through loose, floating ice on the Alaska run, the "St. Helena" was in good company. Both the Cunarder

"Queen Elizabeth 2" and P & O's "Canberra" were employed in carrying the British forces into battle, while B.I.'s "Uganda" served throughout the conflict as a hospital ship.

Everyday on the long passage south the three small ships carried out numerous exercises, designed to bring their ships' companies to full preparedness to counter any possible action on the part of the enemy. Gun drill; small arms practice; refuelling at sea; day and night take-offs and landings by "St. Helena's" helicopter; zig-zagging at flotilla; and every imaginable manoeuvre to ensure that every man on board the three vessels were fully competent to carry out what was required of him.

By June 27 the Flotilla had reached Ascension. After a 48 hour stop to top up with fuel, water and stores, they were on their way again. On July 3 the ships' companies were warned of the possible need to go to defence stations for an indefinite period. Six days later action stations were indeed manned until the three vessels arrived at their destination.

The Flotilla reached Port Stanley on July 10, but before her arrival in the anchorage the "St. Helena" was detached to rendezvous with the Carrier Battle Group to transfer mail. That task completed, the ship was anchored off the port and the two minesweepers were secured alongside their mother ship.

"July 10, 1982: We have been ordered to transfer all remaining mail to HMS "Avenger", and stores to "Avelona Star" and "Geestport". The Hunts (minesweepers) will now prepare for their minehunting role. It is unclear at present whether we will be ordered to operate from another safe anchorage closer to the Hunts' area of operations. At present it appears that the Hunts' first task may be locating and marking the wreck of HMS "Coventry" on the North Coast".

"June 11, 1982: Port Stanley harbour.
Inflate fenders.
HMS "Brecon" and HMS "Ledbury" berth on "St. Helena".
Impending tasks:-
Find the wreckage of HMS "Coventry".
Find the wreckage of HMS "Ardent".
Locate an anchor.
Check the minefield off the entrance to Port Stanley.
Ten mines have yet to be found".
"July 13, 1982: Port Stanley harbour.
Flying stations.
Helicopter 373 + 1st Lieutenant sets up trisponder sites.
On Thursday we shall weigh anchor probably at 0800 and proceed to top up with fresh water from "Fort Toronto" and then diesel from "G.A. Walker".
On completion we shall sail overnight to San Carlos where we wait until the Hunts complete their tasks, possibly two weeks.

RMS ST HELENA (I) at South Georgia, 1982

(Bob Wilson)

Another view of RMS ST HELENA at South Georgia

(Bob Wilson)

97

On completion we shall return to Port Stanley where the Hunts will sweep Port William and Port Stanley approaches".

On July 15 the "St. Helena" duly sailed for San Carlos, where she was to remain at anchor for the next ten days. Then on July 24 the following situation report appeared in the ship's Daily Orders:-

"SITREP: "Brecon" and "Ledbury" had a very good week of hunting. The wreck of HMS "Ardent" was quickly found and surveyed. Very little of the ship remains aft of the Bridge.

HMS "Coventry" was harder to find and HMS "Apollo" called in to search the deeper water, located a contact last night.

The Hunts confirmed the contact as HMS "Coventry" by use of the PAPS (those little yellow submarines!). Diving will be impossible for us because she is in 100 metres of water.

A large part of San Carlos Water has been searched and cleared. Several pieces of ordnance have been counter-mined, including two Sea Cats. "Ledbury" found the wreckage of an aircraft including an ejector seat complete with Argentinian pilot.

A gallon of rum has been given to us by the Royal Fleet Auxiliary "Fort Grange" for 'splicers'!"

And so back to Port Stanley which the three ships reached on July 27. Their next tasks were the minefields at the entrance to Port William, a route survey into Port Stanley, and clearance of any bombs which had missed the airport runway and landed in the sea.

The "St. Helena" remained at anchor in Port Stanley for the next nine days while the Hunts carried out their dangerous mission. July 31 was marked by a visit to the ship for luncheon by His Excellency the Civil Commissioner, Mr Rex Hunt, while that same evening the Senior Naval Officer, Falkland Islands, was a guest at a cocktail party on board, held in the forward lounge, which did duty as the ship's wardroom and senior ratings mess throughout "St. Helena's" Admiralty commission, a curtained partition dividing the Officers from the Chiefs and Petty Officers.

Ten days later on August 6, in the company of the two Hunts, the "St. Helena" left Port Stanley, the Flotilla's destination either Ruggles Bay or Fox Bay. The intention was for the minesweepers to carry out a route survey of Ruggles Bay, and to position a Stena Inspector over the wreck of HMS "Coventry" before the three ships returned to the United Kingdom.

However the C-in-C Fleet ordered their return to Port Stanley for HMS "Brecon" to effect an auxiliary engine replacement, before embarking on the long voyage home, and on August 11 the trio were back at Port Stanley.

Three days later, their task at the Falklands completed, the "St. Helena" in the company of the two Hunts, HMS "Brecon" and HMS "Ledbury", departed Port Stanley en route for St. Helena. And on August 17 the following signal was received by the "St. Helena" from the Senior Naval Officer, Falkland Islands:-

I have been impressed by your team's CAN DO attitude and your ability to get on with the job independently and with a minimum of fuss.
Well done! Bon voyage and safe homecoming!"

On August 24, the day prior to the Flotilla's arrival at Jamestown, the Daily Orders included the following paragraph that marked the end of hostilities as far as RMS "St. Helena" was concerned.

"Now that the situation of Active Service, and with it emergency regulations, have been lifted, it is necessary to revert to normal regulations and procedures. Wasp jollies can no longer be justified. Sorry to all those who missed the opportunity to be lifted by a paraffin parrot!"

On August 25 the RMS "St. Helena" anchored off the jetty at Jamestown to receive a rapturous welcome from the Islanders. The next evening Captain Martin Smith, his ship's officers, and the naval officers serving in the vessel, were the guests of His Excellency the Governor of St. Helena at Plantation House, and on August 27 the small flotilla sailed from Jamestown for Ascension.

Following the ships' arrival off Georgetown all three refuelled from the tanker "Alvega" anchored in the bay, before leaving immediately on August 29 for Gibraltar, where ten days later they were moored alongside in the naval dockyard under the shadow of the Rock.

After an overnight stay for fuel and water the Flotilla left Gibraltar on September 9, on the last leg of their long journey home. Four days after leaving the Rock the three ships were off the coast of Dorset, and "St. Helena's" chopper made a final take-off before landing back at Portland. The Flotilla however continued on passage to the minesweepers' home base at Rosyth.

On the evening of September 15, after HMS "Brecon" and HMS "Ledbury" had made a farewell steam-past the RMS, the three ships anchored for the night in Dalgety Bay before docking the following morning in Rosyth. And it was a great homecoming for the ship's company of the "St. Helena", as they welcomed on board for luncheon those of their families who had travelled north to Scotland to greet the ship on its return from the war zone.

By the month end the RMS was back in Portsmouth for a much needed refit, but although the fighting was over, the mail-ship returned to the Falklands for a further eight months. Only on July 11, 1983 did she enter Falmouth for an extensive refit prior to return to her owners, a year to the day that she had sailed south from Portland to serve her country.

The refit at Falmouth included the removal of the helicopter pad mounted above the Stern Gallery; the complete refurbishing of her accommodation; the restoration of her cargo gear; substantial internal re-plumbing; and the removal of the sophisticated communication equipment installed for the vessel's wartime role; over and above a complete overhaul and refit.

On September 20 the RMS "St. Helena" sailed once more from Avonmouth to resume her scheduled voyages on the Cape run after an absence of 16 months, now proudly displaying a plaque mounted in the lobby outside the Ship's Office, bearing testimony to the important role she had played both during and after the Falklands War.

The "Centaur" arrived in Avonmouth on November 29, 1982, looking resplendent in the livery of the St. Helena Shipping Company, and there were many who hoped that this handsome ship would find a permanent place on the South Atlantic run. At 7,988 gross registered tons she was substantially larger than the RMS, had berths for 188 passengers, and a cargo capacity of 2000 tons.

Apart from carrying double the number of passengers, the "Centaur" was able to offer a wider choice of staterooms, including suites, and she was well equipped with public facilities. These including a Dining Saloon capable of handling all her passengers at one sitting; a Lido Bar overlooking a custom-built swimming pool on the Promenade Deck; the Governor's Bar, a small and intimate room on the deck below the Lido; a forward facing Library and Writing Room; a sizeable shop; a Hairdressing Salon; and perhaps most important of all, a Children's play area, an asset sadly lacking in the RMS "St. Helena".

On paper the "Centaur" was a more than suitable stand-in for the RMS, and had she been in better condition Curnow Shipping would have given serious consideration to purchasing the ship which was available for outright sale.

But the truth was that the "Centaur's" engines driving her twin screws were in poor shape, and evidence of severe corrosion was present in her aluminium superstructure. Furthermore, her hold capacity, which had been designed more for the carriage of livestock rather than general cargo, proved inadequate, and would have been very costly to modify. Finally her cranky stability was a matter for concern.

In view of the vessel's shortcomings Curnow Shipping decided against purchasing the ship, a wise decision in the light of subsequent mechanical breakdowns. But nonetheless "Centaur" more than adequately filled the gap created by the involuntary absence of the "St. Helena", and proved very popular with her passengers.

It was all very sad and disappointing. The "Centaur" had been built in John Brown's famous shipyard on Clydebank for the Blue Funnel Line in 1964 to the highest standards, and had been in every respect a well found vessel. Measuring 480 feet overall, she was powered by two Burmeister and

RMS CENTAUR off Ascension, April 1982   (P. C. Kohler)

Crossing the Line aboard RMS CENTAUR, April 1983

(P. C. Kohler)

Wain diesels developing 16,500 brake horse-power to drive her twin-screws, giving a useful service speed of 18 knots.

But poor maintenance and neglect had left their mark, and while under charter to the St. Helena Shipping Company mechanical breakdowns were frequent. The climax reached before the start of her final round voyage for Curnow Shipping, when preparing to sail from Avonmouth the donkey boiler fell apart, delaying her departure for a further 10 days while repairs were effected.

In terms of the charter, the "Centaur's" Master, deck officers, deckhands, wireless operators, ship's surgeon, engineering officers and engine-room personnel were all provided by the Straits Steamship Company; while the St. Helena Shipping Company supplied the Purser, Catering Officer, catering and cabin staff, as well as a company Master to sail in the vessel as a supernumary to care for the company's interests, and to maintain a close liaison with Porthleven.

After completing her final round voyage to the Islands and the Cape, the "Centaur" left Avonmouth for the last time on October 18, 1983, bound for her home port Singapore, after a year in the South Atlantic trade. With a reasonable compliment of passengers the liner called at the Cape, and at Durban, before proceeding by way of Mauritius to Fremantle in Western Australia.

While at Mauritius the "Centaur" reverted to the livery of the Straits Steamship Company, and it was fitting that the ship should return to her familiar stamping ground sporting the familiar blue funnel with black topping that was a feature of the Blue Funnel Line.

A number of passengers had elected to sail on to Fremantle, and from there to Singapore, while others joined the ship at South African ports. Australians who had previously sailed in the "Centaur" joined the liner at Fremantle, ensuring that there was no empty berths when she left that port on the final leg of her long voyage home to Singapore.

The "Centaur" remained laid up at anchor in bay at Singapore for the next twelve months, until she was purchased by Chinese owners for service in the China Sea named "Hai Long".

The return of the RMS "St. Helena" to her scheduled sailings was a relief to the Management, for suitable as the "Centaur" had been as a stand in for the smaller ship, the difficulties and complexities of managing a vessel in which the only company personnel had been the catering and cabin staff had been manifold, so a return to an all-company manned ship was welcomed by all concerned.

The RMS was quickly back in her regular routine as voyage followed voyage without incident, but on Voyage 35 her ship's company were to be tested to the full in an unexpected mishap that is every Shipmaster's dread, a fire at sea. They had left St. Helena homeward bound on October 27, 1984 with 88 on board, 31 of whom were passengers. A call at Ascension for cargo followed, and at 18.00 on the evening of October 29 the mail-ship was on course for Teneriffe.

Two days later on October 31 an entry in the ship's log, at the change of watch at 20.00, recorded the weather conditions as what could normally be expected when passing through the doldrums. "Wind East-South-East, force 1–2; barometer reading 1009.4; air temperature 26.8°C; sea temperature 28.3°C; visibility clear; a partly cloudy sky; and rippled sea with a low South-Easterly swell". Following dinner that evening some 40 passengers and officers were gathered in the forward lounge to enjoy the night's entertainment, organised in his inimitable way by the Purser Geoffrey Shallcross, with the able assistance of the Assistant Purser Angela Read. At 22.25 as the log recorded, the accommodation lighting began to flicker, attributed by Chief Engineer Bryan Gillott to possible generator trouble.

The Second Engineer Tim Walpole immediately left the cheerful gathering and made his way below, down the forward stairwell to the port entrance to the engineroom. As he opened the door he was faced with thick smoke that barred his entry. Hastily closing the door again Walpole immediately telephoned the Bridge to alert the Officer on Watch, and to get breathing apparatus down to the foredeck.

At the same time, as the accommodation lights went out and the emergency lighting came on, the Chief Engineer realised the main engine had stopped, and that smoke was seeping from under the port side door leading into the engineroom. He immediately set off the fire alarm on A deck, contacted the Bridge by telephone, and instructed the Officer on Watch to sound the general emergency signal.

The RMS "St. Helena" on Voyage 35 was under the command of a relief Master, Captain Mike Underwood, who had joined Curnow Shipping Ltd. six years previously, and had since served as Chief Officer and Master in a number of their ships, He was called to the Bridge just four minutes after the accommodation lights had flickered, and as he stepped through the wheelhouse door the general emergency alarm signal was sounding a swift reaction, under any circumstance, to possible trouble.

As the crew members went about their duties the Purser was mustering passengers in the forward lounge with their lifejackets, warm clothing, or a blanket stripped off their bed.

Meanwhile the Second Engineer had heard calls for help from the engineroom, and going to the port side watertight door assisted in the rescue of the Fourth Engineer who had been overcome by fumes. He was carried on to the foredeck where he quickly recovered and reported the engineroom evacuated. When the Chief Engineer reported to the Master that he intended to flood the engineroom with Carbon Dioxide in an attempt to smother the fire Captain Underwood agreed, and realising that the situation was extremely serious gave the order "withdraw to boats", while instructing the Wireless Officer to broadcast a "Mayday" signal, calling for immediate assistance. The time was 22.44 only 19 minutes after the first indication of trouble below.

While steps were being taken to extinguish the fire, the Purser had prepared the passengers for abandoning ship. He and the Catering Officer Dave Padmore ensured that extra supplies of soft drinks and cigarettes were placed in the ship's two lifeboats, which had been lowered to the level of the Promenade deck, ready for abandoning ship should it prove necessary. Despite the gravity of the situation there was no panic on the part of the passengers, a tribute to the reassuring presence of the Purser and his emergency party.

Upon receipt of the Captain's order "withdraw to boats" all passengers and non-essential crew embarked safely into the two lifeboats under the supervision of the Second Officer, while the Second Engineer, with a Mechanic, re-entered the A deck accommodation area using breathing apparatus, and managed under extremely difficult conditions to flood the engineroom with Carbon Dioxide. This accomplished, the Engineers awaited further developments in the hopes that the blaze had been smothered.

Two vessels, the "Overseas Argonaut" and the "Kittanning", responded to the S.O.S. The first named was 25 miles from "St. Helena's" dead-reckoning position at 22.30 of 5° 26' South, 16° 46', West, while the second ship was a further 55 miles away. When the Master of the "Overseas Argonaut" confirmed his ship was proceeding to the rescue of the "St. Helena" with all despatch, Captain Underwood was able to advise the Master of the "Kittanning" that no further assistance was required, and that unless circumstances deteriorated, he did not intend abandoning his ship.

In the knowledge that the "Overseas Argonaut" would reach the RMS within the next two hours, Captain Underwood was able to reassure his passengers that should the position deteriorate help was at hand, and when the lights of the approaching vessel were sighted the tension relaxed appreciably.

After an hour in the lifeboats, awaiting the order to abandon ship should that prove necessary, passengers were permitted to return to the ship, but for safety were requested to remain on deck. On such a balmy night that was no hardship.

It appeared that the release of the Carbon Dioxide had brought the fire under control, although a thorough inspection below some five hours later revealed hot spots on the engineroom casing bulkheads on all three decks. The emergency fire-pump was then activated with the intention of dowsing any remaining flames, but without success as the fire main riser from the General Service pump was later found to have split. However, by connecting a chain of hoses from the sprinkler pump, the problem was effectively overcome and the affected bulkheads dowsed down.

However, the efforts made to cool the bulkheads down had released quantities of water into the accommodation area, necessitating keeping the passengers overnight in the forward lounge. And by 08.00 the following morning Captain Underwood recorded a 5° list, due to water in the bilges. At 11.00, as the engineroom bulkheads had cooled down considerably, it was considered that the Carbon Dioxide had successfully extinquished the blaze.

Using breathing apparatus the Second Engineer, in the company of the Fourth Engineer, entered the engineroom for an initial recconaissance. They reported no sign of fire, so engineroom personnel commenced the task of restoring services as far as it was possible to do so.

By 16.00 that afternoon the General Service pump riser had been repaired and the fire-fighting water restored to the fire main. The following morning November 2, the situation on board RMS had improved to such an extent that at 10.20 Captain Underwood was able to release the "Overseas Argonaut", which had continued to stand by the drifting mail-ship, as he considered his command was no longer in imminent danger.

Although in the opinion of the Chief Engineer the main engine could be restarted, he advised Captain Underwood that in view of the state of the engineroon it would be imprudent to do so. Furthermore, the supply of Carbon Dioxide had been exhausted in quelling the fire, should another emergency occur. He recommended therefore that a tug be summoned and the vessel be taken in tow.

Captain Underwood concurred and contacted Simon Sugrue at Curnow Shipping's office in Porthleven for his approval, which was readily forthcoming, Action was swift, and by midday Simon Sugrue was able to advise the RMS that the salvage tug "Fairplay IX" was on its way to take the "St. Helena" in tow.

In the interim Bryan Gillott and his Engineers were busy restoring the ship's domestic services, and by that evening sanitary and domestic water were both available, while the main generator was once more in working order.

The "St Helena" remained drifting "not under command" until 09.00 Monday November 5, when the West German tug took her in tow. Although the two nearest ports were Freetown and Monrovia, neither could offer the extensive repair facilities that would be required. The decision was therefore taken to make for Dakar, since the vessel was no longer in immediate danger.

At 11.48 three days later the crippled ship entered the roadstead off Dakar, where two harbour tugs took over the two from the "Fairplay IX". Safely berthed alongside, the St. Helena disembarked her passengers who were flown to England that evening, and began to repair the damage predominantly to the engineroom.

The necessary repairs occupied three weeks, so Voyage 35 effectively terminated at Dakar. Once the "St. Helena" had been inspected and classified as A1 by Lloyds' surveyor she was ready to re-enter service, but instead of returning to Avonmouth she sailed for Cape Town on Voyage 36.

No further mishaps of any consequence tarnished the RMS "St. Helena's" reputation for reliability during the remaining seven years she operated the service. However, prior to the launch of the new "St. Helena" by H.R.H. The Prince Andrew on October 31st 1989, she underwent a further name change, and for her final twelve months of service in the Cape trade sailed as the RMS "St. Helena Island".

In the thirteen years the RMS sailed the Cape run she completed 70 round voyages, albeit Voyage 27, when the ship was under charter to the Ministry of Defence both during and after the Falklands War, occupied rather more than twelve months. In all she steamed some 840,000 miles and her diesel engine consumed 38,009 tons of fuel, in 141017 hours steaming, still with the original pistons, bearing liners, and engine block. She carried approximately 24,000 passengers and 49,000 tons of freight.

Apart from general cargo, the RMS sometimes resembled Noah's Ark carrying a wide variety of animals, sheep, horses, pigs, tortoises, cats, parrots, dogs, bulls, gerbils, hamsters, hens, budgerigars, canaries, goats, peacocks, frogs, cows and eggs in incubators!

And for the statistically minded, her passengers and crew consumed 213 tons of meat; 41 tons of fish; 43 tons of poultry; 190 tons of potatoes; 160 tons of vegetables; 24 tons of sugar; 4 tons of tea; 2 tons of coffee; 21 tons of cheese; 113,616 litres of milk; 5128,400 eggs; and 21 tons of ice-cream. Renamed "Avalon" this gracious old lady briefly embarked on a new career in the Indian Ocean, but sadly was laid up late in 1991 and resold in the summer of 1993.

The first of the "Saints" has made her final curtsey on the Cape run, and a fine new RMS "St. Helena" has taken the stage following her departure for pastures new, but before we are introduced to the new RMS let us make a voyage together southbound for the Islands.

V SOUTHBOUND FOR THE ISLANDS

When Curnow Shipping was awarded the St. Helena contract Avonmouth was selected as the home port for the cargo-liner RMS "St. Helena". The port charges were competitive and the labour force co-operative, while the port was conveniently situated at the mouth of the River Seven, opening into the Bristol Channel. Avonmouth lies to the north-west of Bristol, some seven miles distant from that ancient seaport, no longer an ocean terminal. The port is well serviced by road and rail, while Bristol's airport is within easy reach.

Curnow Shipping's association with the Port authorities at Avonmouth was an amicable one, and was to continue for the thirteen years the first RMS was employed on the Cape run. However, when the second RMS "St. Helena" entered the mail service in November 1990, the decision had already been taken to change her home port to Cardiff in South Wales.

Associated British Ports, the owners of Cardiff Docks, had made Curnow Shipping such an attractive offer it was virtually impossible for them to refuse, so Avonmouth was abandoned in favour of the Port of Cardiff.

Ideally situated as it is on the northern shore of the Bristol Channel, Cardiff has the disadvantage of less direct road and rail links with London and the Midlands for the conveyance of freight, while passengers may find access to the port less convenient than had been the case when joining the ship or disembarking at Avonmouth.

But in a competitive market the financial inducement to move to Cardiff was irresistible, and while the current contract with the Cardiff Port authorities remains in force, the RMS "St. Helena" will become as familiar a sight in her new home port as were the Geest banana boats to the port of Barry, some ten miles to the south-west of Cardiff, before their move to Southampton.

In the latter half of the 19th Century the South Wales Coalfields were flourishing, and apart from domestic demand a large export trade developed. To cater for this export market, construction of the first enclosed dock system began in Cardiff in the 1830's, and on October 19, 1839 the Bute West Dock Basin was officially opened, when an estimated crowd of twenty thousand people watched the steamer "Lady Charlotte" enter the Basin through the lock gates and berth inside.

As export sales of coal increased further docking facilities were required, and sixteen years later the first section of the Bute East Dock was opened to shipping, although the entire project was only completed in 1859. The overseas demand for coal appeared insatiable, and by 1874 the port authorities had responded by converting a tidal harbour, south of the Bute East Dock, into what was named the Roath Basin. And by 1887 the Roath Basin had been connected by a lock to a new Roath Dock.

But despite the extensive additional facilities provided, Cardiff Docks were still unable to cope adequately with the volume of shipping demanded, and yet a further development scheme was undertaken. The last of the Cardiff Docks was officially opened by King Edward VII and Queen Alexandra in 1907, and appropriately enough this final extension to the port was named Queen Alexandra Dock.

By 1907 Cardiff Docks had become the largest coal, exporting port in the world, and in 1913 a record 13.5 million tons were handled. But the outbreak of the First World war in 1914 brought about a decline in the export trade from which the Welsh coal industry never recovered. The development of the Gulf oilfields in the 1920s caused industries in general, and shipping companies in particular, to switch from coal to oil, and the demand for Welsh coal had halved by the time the Second World War broke out in 1939.

In 1922 the Great Western Railway had acquired all the ports in South Wales, including Cardiff Docks, and the port remained under the company's control until the privately owned railway networks in Great Britain were nationalised under the banner of British Rail in 1947. For many years the Department of Transport became the Cardiff Port Authority, but in the 1980's as was the case with Barry Docks, ownership was acquired by Associated British Ports.

The Second World War provided Cardiff Docks with a much needed stimulus, and apart from accommodating units of the Royal Navy, the port was actively engaged in handling the vital foodstuffs, armaments and troops of the Allied Forces convoyed across the North Atlantic. But following the cessation of hostilities the port once again experienced a lean period, so much so that by the end of the 1950s both the Bute West and East Docks were at a standstill. The original dock Bute West was closed down in 1964, while the closure of Bute East was to follow six years later.

Today only the Roath and Queen Alexandra Docks remain in service, but under an active, aggressive management team the fortunes of the port have changed, and the two docks now handle a variety of imports and exports, including iron ore, grain and agricultural products, plant and machinery, manufactured goods, frozen meat from Australasia, and timber from the Baltic.

So it is to the Queen Alexandra Dock that we taxi down from the city centre on sailing day to board RMS "St. Helena". At her berth at 'D'Shed the usual air of activity prevails as stevedores load the last minute consignments of general cargo for the Islands, and bags of Royal Mail are lowered through the after hatch to be safely locked away in the mail room located on 'D'Deck.

At 14.00 passengers begin to embark, after clearance by the Immigration and Customs authorities on the quayside, and organised chaos prevails as cabins are sought and luggage identified, right up to the moment the voice over the public address systems that -

"This ship is about to sail. Would all persons not travelling in the vessel kindly go ashore now, as the gangway is about to be lowered!".

The gangway is lowered to the quay; harbour tugs nuzzle the ship's side awaiting the Pilot's instructions; the lines are let go fore and aft; and taking advantage of the evening tide the mail-ship moves slowly through the lock gates out into the Bristol Channel, as the port echoes to the strain of 'We are sailing', 'Rule Britannia', 'Land of Hope and Glory', and 'Anchors Aweigh'.

Once out in the roadstead the Pilot makes his departure, and we set course to cross the Bristol Channel to the coastline of North Devon. Then passing Ilfracombe to port we make our way towards Hartland Point before another course alteration sees the vessel steaming down the coast of Cornwall, past Land's End and the Longship Lighthouse.

Our first port of call, five days out of Cardiff, is Santa Cruz on the Island of Tenerife. Five days in which to settle in; explore our temporary home for the next almost four weeks; and to get acquainted with our fellow passengers. We eyed one another tentatively as all passengers were mustered in the forward lounge for Boat Drill shortly after departing Cardiff; got to know one another better at the Captain's Cocktail Party on the second night at sea; and by the time the vessel picks up the Spanish Pilot in the approaches to the port of Santa Cruz, we all know each other.

The first RMS originally called at Las Palmas, a practice that continued for almost four years and 21 voyages. It was only on Voyage 22 in 1982 that the change was made to Tenerife, a regular port of call both south and northbound ever since.

Tenerife

Colonised by the Spanish in 1494, Tenerife is one of seven islands collectively designated the Canaries, and although perhaps less familiar to ocean travellers Santa Cruz with its terraced suburbs rising above the city centre, has so much more of interest to offer visitors from abroad than has Las Palmas.

Although the RMS "St. Helena" remains in port only long enough to top up her fuel and water tanks and to embark fresh fruit and vegetables, there is time enough to explore this fascinating city steeped in history and to sample the delicious prawns readily available at any of the many pavement cafes. And as a duty-free port Santa Cruz is a shopper's paradise, with radios, cameras, tape-recorders, binoculars and similar merchandise at a fraction of normal retail prices.

Tenerife is a comparatively large island, fifty miles in length and thirty five miles across at its southern coastline, but because of the time factor there is no real possibility for passengers to explore beyond the city limits.

There is no division between port and city at Santa Cruz, for ships berth virtually in the city centre! a few minutes walk and one is in the Plaza de Espana two sides of which are boarded by the sea, and one by the Post office and an excellent Archeological Museum. On the fourth side a wide rectangular street leads off the square called the Plaza de Candelaria, in which stands the sumptuously appointed Casino to which visitors can obtain temporary membership. But for the passengers of the RMS "St. Helena" time does not permit such indulgence.

Adjoining the harbour lies the Royal Yacht Club which, like the Casino, offers temporary membership to visitors, and where after an aperitif in one of the luxurious lounges a leisurely luncheon can be enjoyed in the dining room, with its uninterrupted vistas of the ocean beyond. Next door stands the Military Museum, of particular interest to English visitors, for the cannon on display is named El Tigre—the tiger—that cost Horatio Nelson his arm in 1797. When British sea-power reigned in the 18th and 19th Centuries, the Government planned the capture of Santa Cruz as a strategic base for the British Fleet, and an assault was launched on the city by Admiral Nelson and his squadron. History records that the Spanish levies snatched a victory denied the might of Napoleonic France. During the fierce engagement Nelson lost not only his arm, but two British ensigns captured from the landing party, which still hang proudly in the cathedral church of La Concepcion.

Off the Plaza de Candeleria runs the Calle del Castillo, most of whose high class shops are owned by Indians, who with their sari-clad womenfolk form a small but colourful section of Santa Cruz society. Strangely enough almost all of them stock the same range of goods, be they knitwear, transistor-radios, cameras or tape records! It is left to the Spaniards to market the more prosaic meat, bread and vegetables.

Another square well worth a visit is the Plaza 25 de Julio, adjacent to the City park. A group of twenty benches in the Plaza are individually decorated with glazed painted tiles each sponsored by a different shop or company, and each advertising what the sponsor offers for sale. A Toy, Shop for example features three dolls reminiscent of the Victorian Age, while vintage car enthusiasts can enthuse over two of the benches donated by the two large motor importing agencies of the time, Fiat and Buick. Each depicts an open tourer with elongated bonnet, running boards, and spoked wheels.

On one side of the Plaza 25 de Jiulio stands the Anglican Church, for the British community resident in Santa Cruz is substantial. The church boasts a garden of which every English visitor can be proud, for behind its high walls one can imagine oneself back in an English Country Village. A number of private homes in this part of the city have lovely gardens, and the splash of vivid colour, mostly bougainvillea, against the white walls of the Spanish styled villas is a memorable sight.

Pride of place however must be conceded to the City Park. Standing in fifteen lush acres it is a treasure to be enjoyed whatever the hour of day or the angle of the sun one can always find a seat in the shade of one or other of the long, leafy avenues that lead to the floral clock just opposite the Calle del Pilar, the ornamental lake, or the zoo alongside the Rambla de General Franco.

A further attractive and interesting feature of the Park is the circular pergola which is partially concealed; and because of the privacy it provides the four seats it contains are frequently occupied by loving couples. When the seats are not occupied each reveals a large glazed painted tile, recording a different phase in the development of the city and the island.

The first tile depicts Guanches, the natives of Tenerife, milling gofia, which is roasted maize flour; herding goats; or wrestling, a traditional sport, against a background of the valley of Orotava. The second shows Guanches looking down on three small sailing ships on the sea far below them and is entitled 'Arrival of the Conquistadores'. In the third picture the Guanches are locked in fierce struggle with the Conquistadores in the Battle of Ancetago while the final tile reveals the 'Riches and civilisation of the Canaries today'. It was probably painted about 1920, depicting as it does an ancient biplane flying over paddle-steamers in the harbour.

Returning to the Plaza de Espana, prior to rejoining the mailship, thirsty sightseers are recommended to drop in at the Cafe Atlantico. Comfortably seated on the cafe terrace one can view the tall column in the centre of the square commemorating those who perished in the Spanish Civil War, a monument as conspicuous as to be visible from the RMS "St. Helena" as she enters the harbour of Santa Cruz.

And on the far side of the Plaza, where the Plaza de Candelaria joins the square, stands an unusual monument in which the Italian sculptor Canova has depicted the Virgin of Candelaria surrounded by the figures of four Guanche Kings. The monument dates back to 1778, when the Spanish Court and its half Italian monarch Charles III were still presiding over an international Empire, and at a time that the Canarios in no way questioned the benefits of Spanish conquest! The four kings in the sculptors are those who showed loyalty to Alonso de Lugo by offering no resistance to the Conquistadores, and are Güimar, Abona, Icod and Daute.

The mail-ship's brief stay is over, and as the RMS "St. Helena" slips her moorings and heads for the open sea we can look back on the mountains that tower above the shoreline. Standing on deck one can discern away to the right the jagged headland of Anaga, and as the Island of Tenerife falls astern of the ship, a tiny white triangle can be seen, the peak of mountain Teide, rising above the intervening heights behind La Laguna and Güimer.

Then as Santa Cruz and the Island of Tenerife fall below the horizon, as our ship sails south on the six day passage to Ascension in the South Atlantic, we can relax and enjoy the sunny warmth of the fair weather route that will eventually bring us into Table Bay.

112

Sundowner off Ascension RMS ST HELENA I, February 1990   (P. C. Kohler)

113

Ascension lies in the middle of the South Atlantic Ocean in latitude 7° 56' South, longitude 14° 25' West, and was discovered by the Portugese navigator Juan da Nova Castella in 1501 while on a voyage to India. Castella named his find Concepcion before proceeding on his passage round the Cape of Good Hope.

Interesting enough, while homeward bound from India, Castella discovered St. Helena, but he failed to call again at his initial discovery in the course of his passage home to Lisbon. In 1503 Concepcion was rediscovered by a fellow Portugese, Alfonso d'Alberquerque, reputedly on Ascension Day, who renamed the island Ascension.

In the course of the next two centuries a number of mariners of different nationalities called at Ascension to slaughter the turtles, which were plentiful, for fresh meat, as well as to rob the seabirds of their eggs to augment their shipboard diet. They in turn put goats ashore for those who were to follow them.

The island was also of value to passing shipping as a 'Post Office' where mail was exchanged by leaving letters in a special bottle at a specific site. This mail-box' was eventually marked by a cross, which by 1693 was known as Cross Hill, a name perpetuated to the present day.

In the course of the 18th Century two famous British explorers are recorded as having visited Ascension. The first was Captain William Dampier on February 22, 1701. Dampier anchored his command "Roebuck" in South West Bay to repair his leaking vessel. After transferring his ship's company and provision to the shore, attempts were made to make the ship seaworthy but to no avail, and the vessel eventually sank at her moorings.

Goat, crab and turtle meats were readily available to the castaways, but of far greater importance to their survival, was the discovery of water on the island to sustain them until they were rescued from their misfortune.

The second British explorer to call was Captain James Cook in his famous HMS "Resolution" in 1775, for the purpose of augmenting his provision with turtle meat.

Surprisingly enough no nation laid claim to Ascension for more than three hundred years until October 18, 1815 when Rear-Admiral George Cockburn annexed the island for Great Britain, and garrisoned it with soldiers as a precautionary measure. The banishment of the defeated Emperor Napoleon to lifetime exile on the Island of St. Helena, 700 miles to the south of Ascension, was the reason for this territorial acquisition, to prevent the French occupying a forward base so strategically placed from which to launch any possible operation to release the imprisoned Bonaparte.

In 1816 the island was commissioned as a 'Stone Frigate' "Ascension". under the command of a Post Captain named Cuppage, attached to the

Cape of Good Hope Squadron of the Royal Navy. Strange to relate the island remained under the control and management of the Royal Navy until 1922 when it was proclaimed a Crown Colony and a dependency of the Island of St. Helena.

Ascension has been aptly described as a 'thirty-three square mile shaped excretion of volcanic waste'. But placed as it is in the South Atlantic Ocean midway between Brazil and West Africa, it became of immense strategic value to the Allied Forces during the Second World War, despite its lack of organic growth and its hostile environment.

When war broke out in 1939 Ascension provided the Allies with an air-base from which reconnaissance aircraft could police the waters of the South Atlantic to deter U-boat attacks on Allied shipping; while the island was invaluable in enabling Allied aircraft, vital to victory in the Western Dersert, to be flown from Brazil to West Africa, refuelling at Ascension en reoute. Then again, Ascension played a vital role as the staging post for the Royal Air Force at the time of the Falklands War.

Shared as the island now is with the United States, Ascension will remain of great strategic value to the Western Alliance well into the 21st Century. The extensive facilities of the Wideawake Airfield, with its substantial establishments of both Royal Air Force and United States Air Force personnel and equipment, are testimony to the important role the island plays in global strategy.

But to return to the 19th Century. The death of Napoleon ended Ascension's importance in preventing a French incursion to secure their Emperor's freedom, and more than a century was to elapse before the island regained its strategic value, other than as a Wireless relay station.

In 1899 the Eastern Telegraph Company established themselves on Ascension when extending the underwater cable, which until then had been laid only as far as the island of St. Helena from its starting point in Cape Town's Table Bay. Thereafter the link was extended to the Cape Verde Islands, then on to England. A further cable linked Ascension with the British Colony at Sierra Leone, enabling Freetown to maintain a direct link with Whitehall via the island.

Over the years, between the naval personnel and the civilian cable staff resident on Ascension, a small community developed. The settlement was named Georgetown, but was known more familiarly by the island populance as Garrison. And with their world-wide experience of colonisation, the small British community did manage, despite the arid terrain, to bring a degree of civilisation to Ascension. This was a major accomplishment as Ascension Island is an extinct volcano, placed on the crest of an abysmal rocky seam known as the Mid-Atlantic Range, which, in comparison to her southern sister St. Helena, is of comparatively recent origin. St. Helena is one of the oldest oceanic islands known to man.

Ascension has also been aptly described as 'Hell with the fire put out!' It resembles an enormous slagheap with ash, piles of cinders, and frozen lava of knife edge sharpness. Harsh and unattractive, the island is still subjected to periodic seismic tremors, at times accompanied by emissions of sulphur gas and the 'plop' of miniature mud and boiling water geysers; a clear indication that the volcanic activity beneath the hard surface crust is by no means yet dead.

Today Ascension is governed in theory by an Administrator, responsible to his senior colleague on the Island of St. Helena. In fact his duties are confined to control of the island's small Police force; the magistrate's Court; and establishing the weekly exchange rate for the St. Helena pound, which comprises the local currency.

The island's Civil Administration is now shared equally with the British Broadcasting Corporation, which maintains an important relay station housing no fewer than six Shortwave Transmitters, broadcasting in the World Service in a variety of languages.

The Administrator resides in a one-time naval sanatorium, sited on the island's sole prominence, Green Mountain, the only area of vegetation on an otherside barren surface. Ascension boasts no native population, for every person on the island is a transient worker.

Apart from the R.A.F. and U.S.A.F. personnel, and the staff of the BBC already referred to, there is a large colony of Cable and Wireless employees and their families, responsible for the efficient operation of this major facility. And then there is the labour force, all recruited on a contract basis from St. Helena, and only resident on Ascension for a twelve-month period until replaced by fellow St. Helenans on a shift for shift basis

The Falklands campaign injected new life, and even greater significance to Ascension. Without its facilities Britain would have been hard pressed to maintain the flow of aircraft, men and material to the forces based on South Georgia, and the shore facilities were expanded and developed accordingly.

Apart from the service personnel, the B.B.C and the Cable and Wireless staff, Ascensions today also accommodated the Compoisite Signals Organisation, and inteligence operation set up by the Americans to monitor signals traffic world-wide, not only through the ether, but via the numerous communication satellites in orbit around the earth.

Such a significant community must therefore be supplied by sea. Surprisingly enough therefore, notwithstanding the extensive development of runways and shore establishments, no effort has been made to improve the landing facilities, which to all intents and purposes are no different to what was in existence a century ago!.

Replenishment tankers, loaded with vital cargoes of oil, aviation fuel, and even fresh water, still lie some miles off shore at anchor, discharging their liquid freights by way of underwater pipelines. Bulk stores must needs be transported to the antiquated quay in motor-powered lighters, but unloading is only possible in the most favourable weather conditions, with a calm sea and minimul swell.

The mail-ship, the island's only regular sea-link with England, carrying amongst its general freight for Ascension those vital necessities for the NAAFI canteen ashore, has on a number of occasions been compelled to continue on its passage to St. Helena without landing such precious commodities as beer, spirits, and a variety of other refreshments!

Weather conditions permitting, the RMS "St. Helena" will anchor a mile off Georgetown jetty, discharge such cargo consigned to Ascension, and disembark her passengers by launch for a run ashore. Regrettably, because the island is a top security area, such excursions are confined to a guided tour by minibuses. Visitors to the island are discouraged and as a consequence there is still no hotel on Ascension, nor do facilities exist for the entertainments or refreshment of the mail-ship, other than the bus tours along prescribed routes.

The strict security measures enforced therefore preclude any opportunity of viewing the indigenous wild life on the island. Bleak and barren for the most part, Ascension's natural animal populance consists only of rats, which found their way ashore from passing ships, and cats introduced by the Royal Navy in an effort to exterminate the former! The cats however preyed instead on the vast sea-bird colony, and very soon ran wild.

Today their long legged descendants still roam the fields of clinker and lava, while the rats emerge during the dark hours to scavenge. The goats introduced by passing mariners became a nuisance, and were finally eradicated in 1944, while other than a few dozen donkeys the only remaining animal life are land crabs, a small lizard, and a species of gecko.

But if Ascensions is almost devoid of animal life, birds are in abundance, while the waters surrounding the island team with fish and turtles. Were permission forthcoming, Ascension would be an angler's and bird-watchers paradise. Blackfish, a most voracious eater abounds, but is itself inedible. However bonito, barracuda, albacore, tuna and wahoo are there for the taking, while dolphins and porpoises in pursuit of flying fish can be seen in large schools. The added presence of blue sharks makes bathing a hazard, other than off one or two beaches where their tell-tale dorsal fin can be spotted early enough for safety.

At one time Ascension was the breeding ground for millions of sea-birds as the guano-covered rocks in low lying parts of the island clearly testify. But the introductions of cats by the Royal Navy in 1815 effectively, if inadvertently, dominated the wild life pattern, and today only the Wide-awake terns retain their traditional low lying nesting sites in any quantity.

However on Boatswain Bird Island, which lies some two cables off the western coastline of Ascension, the Ascension frigate-bird can be seen, vicious in appearance and with the adult male boasting a wing-span of up to six feet. Their nesting sites are shared with the white and brown bobbies; the re-billed and yellow-billed botswain birds; the Madeiran petrel; and the black noddy.

Surprisingly enough the development of Ascension as a major air-field; the rash of radar dishes and wireless masts that mark the island's

RMS ST HELENA I in James Bay, St Helena, February 1990

(P. C. Kohler)

importance as a cable, radio and missile tracking station; along with the thousands of service personnel required for their effective operation, have in no way driven the sea-birds from their traditional breeding grounds.

Strangely no detailed study of the teeming marine life in the precincts of Ascension has ever been published, other than that of the giant green turtle. It was the turtle that first attracted the notice of mariners to the island as a source of fresh meat; for slow-moving on land as they are, the turtles were no match for determined sailors and they were slaughtered in their hundreds.

After the British Occupation in 1815 turtle 'turning' became a lucrative commercial enterprise, for apart from providing the resident garrison with fresh meat, the soldiers on neighbouring St. Helena were victualled, as were passing merchantmen and ships of the Royal Navy. Turtle ponds for storing live specimens in sea water were built at the time, to ensure a constant supply for the active market that existed, and two such ponds are still in existence at Long Beach.

Thousands of these docile creatures were butchered to meet the market demand, both local and overseas, before the practice was stopped as recently as 1930. Now, between January and April each year, during the dark hours, English Bay, South West and North East Bays, Deadmans Beach and Long Beach are the undisturbed scene of turtle egg laying.

Each female lays approximately one hundred eggs which take sixty days to hatch, releasing the five-inch baby turtles which unhesitatingly scamper straight to the sea. And although mortality is high, because of natural predators, a number do survive to adulthood. Now monitored by scientists of the University of Florida, it is hoped that the turtle will no longer be an endangered species.

Our brief visit to Ascension is over, and as the RMS "St. Helena" heads south for her port of registry, we are left to contemplate on the barren bleakness of this volcanic wilderness, which studded with radar dishes and tracking equipment resembles the set up of a science-fiction film.

St. Helena

Two days after leaving Ascension the mail-ship lies anchored off St. Helena. After discharging the balance of her cargo, the RMS will embark 'Saints' those contracted to work for a twelve month stint on Ascension and return. Safely disembarked, their places on board will be taken by the relieved labour force returning home for a well-earned break.

Consequently all passengers must be landed at Jamestown for an eight-day sojourn while the Island Ferry run is completed, and in the course of our voyage the ship's Purser has made the necessary arrangements regarding accommodation. The majority choose to stay at the Consulate Hotel in the town centre, a convenient location, or the smaller nearby Wellington House. But for the more adventurous the small, self-catering country inn at Woodlands, some five miles out of town, is a wise choice, particularly in the summer months when Jamestown can be oppressively hot.

St. Helena lies in latitude 16° 00' South, longitude 5° 45' West, and covers an area of 47 square miles, being approximately ten miles long and six miles wide. it is wholly volcanic in origin, and is rugged and mountainous, its highest peak rising 2,697 feet above sea level.

Historically the tenure of St. Helena falls into four distinct phases. It was discovered by Portugese navigators in 1502, and remained a Portugese possession until 1587. Over the next seventy years its ownership was disputed by the maritime nations of Europe until, in 1659, the island was annexed by the English East India Company, which assumed responsibility for its administrations and defence.

During the following one hundred and seventy-five years St. Helena prospered, becoming an important staging-post for the East India men on their lengthy voyages to and from the sub-continent by way of the Cape of Good Hope. Fresh food and water were in abundant supply, and the future of the islanders seemed assured. But in 1834 the East India Company was no longer the powerful maritime force it had once been, and in that year St. Helena was declared a Crown Colony. The island continues to be governed from Whitehall to the present day.

The influence of the East India Company on the development of the island can be seen in the buildings, as well as in both the civil and military engineering projects undertaken during the period of their administration, and it is estimated that 80% of all present day structures were completed during the Company's stewardship.

Rising majestically out of the sea, St. Helena is the loneliest major outpost of what was once known as the British Empire, a 'pinpoint of inaccessibility and unbelievably remote' as it has been described. And that apt description holds good today, for St. Helena cannot by nature provide the facilities for the constructions of an airport, while no harbour exists, only a primitive jetty.

The island reached its peak of prosperity between the years 1815 and 1821, when Napoleon Bonaparte was a prisoner in exile, and a substantial military presence added greatly to the local population. But following the Emperor's demise the garrison was to a large extent withdrawn. The advent of the steamship, and the opening of the Suez Canal, led to a further decline in the fortunes of St. Helena as it was no longer considered of strategic value to Great Britain, which today holds little regard for the welfare of the island populance.

Like so many of the great Atlantic Islands St. Helena combines mountainous terrain with fertile valleys. Trees grow in abundance, the soil is rich, and water is plentiful. But although once a large scale producer of fresh meat and vegetables for passing sailing ships, St. Helena is no longer even self-sufficient in supplying its own domestic requirements. Today the vital supplies of potatoes, onions, and foodstuffs of every variety, are brought to the island from Cape Town every second month by the mail-ship on its northbound passage back to the United Kingdom.

At a later date, in the 1870's St. Helena became a significant exporter of sisal, but the development of man-made fibres sealed the fate of this once flourishing trade, and today barely thirteen square acres of New Zealand flax remains.

It is illogical that the island populace should depend upon imported provisions when the land should be capable of supplying almost all its needs, from fruit and vegetables to milk and meat. That this can be done on St. Helena with a little effort was evidenced by the Achievements in this regard by Joyce and Cyril Allwood during their period of residence.

At their small country inn Woodlands, situated on the high land above Jamestown, they grew their own extensive range of fruit and vegetables; raised their own pigs and poultry; processed their own ham, bacon and sausages; established a regular supply of milk and beef. What the Allwoods accomplished in a comparatively short space of time, could be a pattern for the rehabilitation of the island as an agricultural community, if only official encouragement was forthcoming from the Foreign and Commonwealth Office in London. But the story of St. Helena is a sad tale of isolation, poverty and decay, despite the loyality of the proud and friendly islanders to the Mother country, and the lush beauty of their habitat.

The island capital, Jamestown, is situated on the north-west coastline, on a small bay sheltered from the prevailing south-east Trade Winds. The mail-ship anchors half a mile offshore, unloading her anxiously awaiting cargo into lighters. Landing is a hazard other than in a flat calm, as the ground swell, rolling in from the Atlantic, generally results in a rise and fall at the landing steps of up to six feet every thirty seconds.

Described as a place 'with only one entrance and no exit' St. Helena has in its capital Jamestown a unique example of 18th Century architecture, readily accessible to a visitor landing at the port. A short walk from the landing steps along the seafront brings one to the Castle entrance. Crossing a narrow bridge over the now dry Castle moat, one passes through a portcullis'd gate in a wall twelve feet thick on to what is known as the Lower Parade.

The old Castle stands in this square, with white-washed walls and still displaying the coat of arms of the Honourable East India Company. Leading off the square up the main street stand two rows of Regency houses, with iron trellises and sash windows, while beyond the Castle Courtyard lie the island Courts and a pleasant public park.

It is claimed that there is more history crammed into the tiny town of Jamestown than in any part of the British Commonwealth. On the right of the Lower Parade, opposite the Castle and alongside the small Prison, stands St. James Church, built when the East India Company annexed the island more than three centuries ago. In its churchyard the majority of St. Helena's aristocracy are buried, the Benjamins, Thomases, Hudsons, Youngs, Greens and Solomons, to name but a few of the oldest families.

The first Solomon settled on St. Helenas in 1790, and today his enterprise, and the dynasty he founded, are to be seen in the family's continued dominance of the island's economy. It is almost impossible, it seems, to conduct any business transaction in Jamestown other that with Solomon & Co., who own the brewery; the Consulate Hotel; run the banking service; supply the provender; are the main Government trading agency; and are sole agents for the St. Helena Shipping Co., the only escape route to the outside world, and the service they formerly provided for the Union-Castle Line.

Jamestown lies at the base of a valley flanked by two immense ridges of basalt, Munder's Hill with its ruins of two batteries in the east, and Ladder Hill, where the old fort, barracks, observatory and signal station were built, to the west. A narrow road, winding its dangerous path for two miles up the valley, provides access to the interior of the island; while for the dedicated tourist access to the old fort from the two below is provided up Jacob's ladder, a unique stairway comprising seven hundred stone steps, a formidable challenge.

A feature of the colonisation of St. Helena is the mixture of races, resulting in the present 'Saints' as the islanders proudly describe themselves! Cockneys from London, following the Great Fire in 1666, sailed in considerable numbers to start a new life on the island, and were responsible for its early development as an agricultural community of some significance. With the increased flow of shipping calling for water and fresh provisions the community grew, as slaves, Chinese labourers, Malayans, Madagascans, Indians, and more Englishmen and the inevitable Scot arrived. A further increase in the polyglot populance was of course provided through the influx of soldiers, comprising the extensive garrison stationed on St. Helena at the time of Napoleon's exile.

Notwithstanding the valuable traffic in water and fresh provisions for passing shipping, undoubtedly the most important single event to boost the early prosperity of St. Helena was Napoleon's exile on the island. Not only was a substantial garrison installed to prevent possible attempts by the French to gain his release, but Ascension Island and Tristan da Cunha were similarly manned both perforce provisioned from St. Helena.

Although the security forces were drastically reduced following the death of the French Emperor, a number of soldiers and marines elected to remain on St. Helena, forming the basis of settlement.

When the Honourable East India Company relinquished control of St. Helena to the British Crown, it was written by one historian that of all the disasters in the island's history this was in all probability the worst. None of the 'Saints' wanted the change, and were adversely affected by the Crown's action in dismissing long-serving Company officials while substantially reducing financial assistance from London. As a result the stature of the Colony was lowered and hundreds of 'Saints' left the island for good, settling in the Cape colony or returning to England.

122

Ideally isolated for the purpose, St. Helena resumed its previous role as an open prison when, following his defeat by British forces after a series of Kaffir Wars in the 1880s, the Chief of the Zulus and his entourage were exiled from Natal to the island. Then again, at the turn of the century and following their defeat by the British in the second Boer War, some 6,000 Boer prisoners of war were held on St. Helena, and the garrison forces increased accordingly.

During both periods of detention the populace thrived in a stimulated economy, but following the repatriation of the detainees the previous Government's disinterest in, and neglect for the welfare of the islanders swiftly reappeared.

To be fair to the British Government, during the second half of the 19th Century various agricultural experiments were carried out on St. Helena, but in each instance, despite favourable indications, the projects were abandoned, possibly through lack of application. Coffee was tried but discontinued, despite a guaranteed market by London merchants. Then for a brief period Cinchona replaced the coffee, and quinine was successfully exported until the then Governor lost interest, and the plantation was abandoned to nature.

The only success achieved in agriculture on a large scale was New Zealand flax, probably because once established the plants required little cultivation, and thousands of acres were covered with flax which thrived in the temperate climate. The first mill to process the sisal was constructed by the Colonial and Fibre Company in 1874, while during the next twenty years seven more mills were built, culminating, in a rope factory in the early 1920s.

At its peak the flax industry employed 400 men, selling its product to the British Post Office, and to a lesser extent to the British Admiralty. But the island's reliance on predominantly a single buyer was to bring about the collapse of what had been a highly successful venture. The Post Office switched to man-made fibres, while the world market price for flax and hemp dropped so dramatically that St. Helena could no longer find a market for its output, and yet another agricultural failure was recorded.

At the same time the island's role as a coaling station for ships of the Royal Navy came to an end, as the Navy switched to oil fuel. As a consequence the strategic value of St. Helena to the British Fleet was no longer of any importance, resulting in the remaining members of the already reduced garrison being withdrawn as no longer necessary. The two events had a profound effect on the well-being of the island community.

The waters surrounding St. Helena are noted for a wide variety of game fish, including tuna on a generous scale, attracting angling enthusiasts from as far afield as South Africa, and in this one source of food the island has always been self-sufficient. In recent years a small Fish Canning factory has been established in Jamestown, and trial exports of canned tuna have been highly acceptable. If necessary finance is forthcoming from Whitehall to allow increased production to meet a growing market demand, this new venture could provide much needed employment for the island populace.

At the present time, apart from the small labour force working the cannery, the only opportunity open to those male islanders remaining on St. Helena is employment by the Government on low paid menial tasks, such as road maintenance, cleansing services, etc. As a consequence the 'Saints, are a poor community. A limited number of men and women are employed as crew aboard the RMS "St. Helena", but the great majority of the male population are recruited on a contract basis to provide the labour force on neighbouring Ascension Island.

Although the Foreign and Commonwealth Office maintains that its financial aid to St. Helena averaged £1000 per head of population by the late 1980s. the truth is that most of this financial subsidy is disbursed in wages, and by British standards on a very low scale. There had been one major source of outside income for the 'Saints' and that was the Tourist Trade, for as a tourist attraction St. Helena has much to offer. Excellent deep-sea fishing; a beautiful countryside; island handicrafts; and so much of historical interest, especially the house occupied by Napoleon during his island exile, are major attractions. And in Jamestown itself, boasting some 1,500 inhabitants, the small but interesting museum bears testimony to the island's rich past.

From the commencement of the Cape mail service well over a century ago St. Helena enjoyed a thriving tourist trade, for as part of the mail contract it was obligatory for a vessel of the Union-Castle Line to call twice monthly at the island. That service was provided up to early 1962, when the Intermediate liners were withdrawn from service. Thereafter regular contact was maintained by two mail passenger liners on a some-what less frequent basis and this from 1965–1967 on a bimonthly basis by the "Capetown Castle", supplemented by cargo vessels. From 1968 contact with the island was maintained by the company's two fast freighters operating in the mail service, but with accommodation for only twelve passengers. So apart from a very occasional call by a cruise liner, once Union-Castle withdrew their passenger ships the tourist trade to all intents and purposes, came to an end.

Even the establishment towards the end of 1977 of the St. Helena Shipping Company to provide a regular service between the United Kingdom, Ascension Island, St. Helena and Cape Town, has done little to assist tourism, as the RMS "St. Helena" makes only twelve calls at the island annually, six outward bound for Table Bay and six homeward bound for England. Furthermore priority is rightly accorded St. Helenans travelling to and from the United Kingdom, and the limited number of through passengers who do visit the island are no substitute for the lost trade.

More's the pity, for St. Helena can boast of two contrasting buildings, one of modest appearance but great historical value, and the other a unique architectural gem. Longwood, the residence occupied by Napoleon Bonaparte is now a museum, with the house and its contents just as they were when the French Emperor lived there until the time of his death in 1821. In a gesture of goodwill, the land on which the building stands was donated to the French nation; and the interests of the Republic are in the care of an Honorary French Consul, who supervise the care and maintenance of the house and garden over which the Tricolour proudly flies!

The second treasure is Plantation House, where the island Governors have resided since the mansion was built by the East India Company in 1792. Set in spacious surroundings Plantation House is considered one of the loveliest homes still available to senior British diplomats. The Governor still holds court in this gracious building, and the famous St. Helenan tortoises still occupy the front lawn. Jonathan, assessed by experts as not less that 250 years old, was in residence at Plantation House at the time of Napoleon's exile, and although now blind remains otherwise in good health.

A magnificent library was added to the original mansion by the Governor at the time of Napoleon's captivity, Sir Hudson Lowe, and the residence, with its polished oak floors and mahogany tables, silver salvers and Spode china bearing the Royal Cypher, ensures gracious living reminiscent of the last century. As a Deputy Governor, occupying Plantation House in the absence of His Excellency on home leave, is said to have commented 'the pay is rotten as you well know, but did you ever see such a perfect place as this?'

St. Helena's isolation has unquestionably contributed to the preservation of the Imperial image, and the panoply of Empire so evident to a visitor. In the 1980s a Colonial police officer commanded the local constabulary, and by marrying a 'Saint' ensured his unqualified acceptance into the island community.

Then there is the Bishop of St. Helena who presides over the smallest diocese in the Anglican Church, although stretching as it does as far afield as Ascension Island and Tristan da Cunha, his see is one of the largest in the area. Until recent years the Bishop of St. Helena was resident in Cape Town, visiting his flock annually by courtesy of the Royal Navy. But today, as is right and proper, he lives on the island and conducts his Service in the Cathedral, which was prefabricated in England and brought to St. Helena by sea for erection.

Other direct links with 'Home; include the detachments of Sea Scouts, Boy Scouts and Girl Guides; the annual Armistice Day Parade; and the mandatory Agricultural Show. And wherever the Union Jack is flown there is, of course, cricket!. Played on St. Helena on a miniature ground, the only level area on the island, perched precariously on a small plateau above steep ravines surrounding the playing area, the oval is uniquely situated. So it is not altogether surprising that an enthusiastic fielder, running backwards to take a catch on the boundary, should unhappily fall to his death. With true British phlegm his demise was entered in the score-book as 'Retired dead'!

And along with the panoply of Empire is the 'Saints' obvious affection for the Royal Family, and few homes fail to boast a picture of Her Majesty; The Queen Mother; Prince Charles; and since his recent visit to St. Helena, the Duke of York. Apart from officially opening the new High School on the island Prince Andrew forged a further direct link with St. Helena by naming and launching the new mail-ship RMS "St. Helena" in Aberdeen in October 1989.

The lack of opportunity to find suitable employment on St. Helena has led to a growing desire on the part of the younger generation to look to Great Britain, but the chances for jobs in the United Kingdom are slim indeed. A basic difference between the citizens of the island and Great Britain is one of nationality.

Unlike the Falklanders and the Gibraltarians, the 'Saints' are not considered Britons by the British Government. Although St. Helena is a Crown Colony under the rule of the British Parliament the 'Saints' are denied the privilege of being British citizens. This attitude on the part of Whitehall is difficult to understand, and the resulting disadvantage to the islanders is very real, prohibiting them the right to journey to the United Kingdom to seek employment in the British Isles.

As the noted South African author, the late Lawrence Green, wrote of the 'Saints' 'these are not primitive tribesmen or coolies. They are a unique and truly multi-racial community of considerable natural intelligence and loyalty.'

The present ruling by Westminster is all the more difficult to comprehend in the light of a Charter, written in the name of King Charles II, the original document carefully preserved in the Castle of Jamestown. Inter alia it reads:-

"We do for us, our heirs and successors, declare . . . that all and every person being our subject which do or shall inhabit within the said port or island, and every their children and posterity which shall happen to be borne within the precincts thereof, shall have and enjoy all liberties, franchises, immunities, capacities, and abilities, intents and purposes as if they had been abiding and borne within this our realm of England, or in any of our domains . . .

In simple English the 'Saints' are, by ancient right, as British as had they been born in Cheltenham or Cardiff, in Glasgow or in Gloucester, so for what valid reason have their rights been denied them?

As recently as 1984 the cause of the islanders was debated in the House of Lords, at which protagonists for the 'Saints', such as Lord Buxton and Lord Cledwyn spoke with eloquence and feeling on the sad fate of those who inhabited 'this most enchanting island', and pointing out the poverty and neglect. But to no avail as the Government reiterated their intention to leave the law governing their immigration policy unchanged.

It is of interest to note therefore, that of Great Britain's remaining Colonies, only the Falklands and Gibraltar enjoy the privilege of total national equality. However, of the remainder Hong Kong, peopled to all intents and purposes by aliens, is likely at the time of writing to have full rights of British citizenship granted to some 250,000 Hong Kong citizens!

An extended and energetic campaign has been waged by the island's Anglican Synod on behalf of the 'Saints' and their right to British Citizenship, also without success. their case for the islanders was strengthened following a detailed survey which revealed that even if the 'Saints' were granted proper British passports only about 800 would leave St. Helena to settle and find employment in the British isles. 'Hardly a flood' in the words of one islander. 'You've nothing to be a 'fear'd of!'

The media has been outspoken in its criticism of the Government for its treatment of St. Helena, and for its neglect for the welfare of the island populace, as a few simple newspaper headlines indicate:-

"Black outlook—Colonial Office largely responsible".
"A Cinderella".
"Hard Times on forgotten Island".
"Famous Island the World has forgotten".

But there has been no change of heart at Whitehall. Lethargy at the Island Desk in London has been blamed for the singular lack of concern shown by the Foreign and Commonwealth Office for the welfare of the Island and its people. A recent Governor, John Massingham, instanced delays, often running into months, for a simple request to be answered, or even acknowledged! And on one occasion, when ten islanders were injured in a serious bus accident on Christmas Eve, the then Governor was unable to make contact with London for seven days, while the best part of a month elapsed before a doctor arrived from the United Kingdom to render medical assistance.

To put it bluntly, successive British Governments of both political parties have little to be proud of in their administration of St. Helena and its loyal populace. Poor decisions, lack of interest, and in particular a restricted Budget, have characterised British rule up to the present time. But life continues on an unmistakably British pattern on the island, as it has done for the past three centuries. Undoubtedly it will continue into the future, even though times will get harder and living conditions more difficult, because even in adversity, the 'Saints' are a happy and gregarious community.

For the visitor St. Helena continues to be an island paradise; and isolated haven of peaceful existence in a troubled world. Those travellers who are fortunate enough to take passage in the mail-ship RMS "St. Helena" can be assured of a warm welcome from the islanders, as well as the opportunity of exploring this still unspoilt treasure-chest of history. Conditions may appear primitive to denizens of the outside world, but life on St. Helena has a special charm of its own, placid and unhurried.

Entertainment may be sparse and facilities limited, but for the visitor seeking a refuge from the hurly burly of city life St. Helena has a great deal to offer.

Our eight day sojourn on St. Helena comes to an end as the mail-ship returns to her anchorage in the bay off Jamestown, and Solomon's motor launch ferries us and our baggage back to the ship. Our voyage is still far from over, as for the next five days we will be on passage to Table Bay. Once in the approaches to the port, we will pick up a Pilot before berthing alongside in Cape-Town's Duncan Dock, nestling at the foot of picturesque Table Mountain.

Once a year however, when it is high summer south of the equator, the mail-ship's schedule is amended to include a call at the remote Tristan da Cunha, 1,200 miles south-south-west of St. Helena, and like Cape Town five days steaming before we make our landfall.

Tristan da Cunha

Tristan da Cunha is the principal island of a group of three, and lies in latitude 37° 5′ south, longitude 12° 17′ west in the South Atlantic Ocean. It boasts a community of some 300 islanders on its 38 square miles, and is almost circular in shape. The other two islands, Inaccessible and Nightingale, are very much smaller in size and uninhabited.

Tristan is the cone of a volcano, resting on a base the sides of which are steep cliffs plunging between 1,000 and 2,000 feet into the sea. Only in the north-western corner of the island is there a plateau at the foot of these cliffs that is habitable, and the lives of all the islanders are centred in this area. The settlement is named Edinburgh, after Prince Alfred, Duke of Edinburgh, who visited Tristan in 1867.

The crater at the summit of the 6,760 foot Queen Mary's Peak contains a lake, while a large number of subsidiary volcanic vents are scattered around the lower slopes of the mountain, thought to be extinct. In October 1961 however, one such vent became active, and because of its close proximity to the settlement the entire population had to be evacuated. The islanders were taken to the United Kingdom and given shelter until the danger had passed. And despite the lonely existence Tristan has to offer, almost every Tristan da Cunhan opted to return to their island homes the following year, when it was considered safe to do so.

Tristan da Cunha was discovered in 1506 by the Portugese navigator Admiral Tristao da Cunha, but the first landing on the island was delayed until 1643, and was made by a party of Hollanders. No settlement was established however until Great Britain claimed the island in 1816, as part

RMS ST HELENA I en voyage Tristan da Cunha to Cape Town, February 1990   (P. C. Kohler)

of their ocean-wide defence strategy when Napoleon was held in exile on the island of St. Helena. A garrison was established adjacent to Hottentot Point, the site of the settlement today, and a fortified outpost was constructed.

Only twelve months after the garrison had been landed on Tristan the soldiers were withdrawn, and the island should have once again been uninhabited. However a Scots corporal William Glass and two colleagues elected to remain on the island, and the story of present day Tristan da Cunha stems from that moment.

Glass had with him his coloured wife from Cape Town, and the first of a large family, while during the next ten years various sailors, deserters or castaways, came to the island and either remained or left again as opportunity offered. But in 1827 five women were brought to Tristan from St. Helena as wives for those who had remained on the island, and a small community was established.

Although Great Britain claimed Tristan da Cunha in 1816, it was 1876 before being formally declared to be British territory. In January 1938 this group of three islands, together with Gough Island some 200 miles south-south-east of Tristan, became like Ascension dependencies of St. Helena for administrative purposes.

The summit of Queen Mary's Peak is bleak, and is frequently snow-capped between June and October, but the lower slopes of the mountain, below 5,000 feet, are fertile and fed by numerous springs and streams. With a temperate climate and a moderate rainfall evenly distributed over the island, the islanders have no problem in providing for their simple needs

Potatoes are their staple food, while cattle and sheep thrive on more than adequate grazing, although shelter from the gale force winds which generally prevail is a necessity to ensure their survival. But the basic industry for the entire community is fishing, and an abundance of mackerel, snoek, and many other varieties of fish are available for home consumption.

To fish the waters beyond extensive beds of kelp which encircle Tristan some two cables from the coastline, the islanders developed the Tristan Longboat. 25 feet in length and constructed from a frame of driftwood covered with oiled and painted canvas. it is an interesting fact that the Tristan Longboat is very similar to those in use at Pitcairn Island in the Pacific.

Prior to the Second World War Tristan da Cunha was so isolated that more than a year might elapse before a ship would call with stores and mail. The initiative of a Royal Naval Officer however, the Reverend C.P. Lawrence, brought about a minor industrial revolution on the island, and a marked improvement in the living standard and well-being of the islanders. The Chaplain had been resident on Tristan during the Second World War when a meteorological and wireless station was erected on the island, manned and operated by the Royal Navy. Through his interest and enthusiasm a South African company, South Atlantic Islands Development Corporation established a factory for canning in 1948 and later freezing, crayfish tails. This provided employment on the island for the first time, and much needed revenue from exports of the processed product to Cape Town.

Unfortunately during the volcanic eruption in 1961 the fish cannery was buried under lava, while the landing beaches were virtually obliterated. But as is so often the case, out of a misfortune benefits are derived. In this instance a tongue of lava had created a natural breakwater to the east of Hottentot Point, which enabled a small harbour to be constructed, and this was completed in 1967. The previous year the Development Corporation had opened a new and larger fish processing factory, and the islanders were back in business again.

A second Cape Town based company, Tristan Investments (Pty) Ltd., operates a shipping service between Tristan da Cunha and Cape Town, with the trawler "Atlantic Isle" making regular calls to transport the processed fish products to the world markets.

The income of the island is now derived from the annual royalty paid by the Development Corporation, based on its profits from the fish industry, from the sale of stamps to the world's philatelists; and with development aid forthcoming from the British Government for specific projects. Consequently the small settlement at Edinburgh can now boast a well-equipped modern school; a Government office block; a small hospital; a concrete road round the settlement; and improved sea defences. Furthermore, the islanders' crofts are now equipped with running water, indoor sanitation, and electricity provided by the fish factory.

A resident Administrator has been appointed, responsible to his senior colleague on St. Helena. There is the Manager of the fish factory, who is also responsible for the supervision of any island development projects; a Treasurer; a Superintendent of Posts and Telegraphs, responsible for the island's radio station; a Minister of the Church; and two School Teachers, all of whom provide Tristan with the necessary officials for Local Government.

An Island Council, comprised of eight elected members, now runs the island's affairs, chaired by the Administrator, who is empowered to appoint three additional councillors. Usually these co-opted councillors are the Chaplain; the Assistant Factory Manager; and the holder of the title 'Chief Islander'. Chief Islander supercedes the old title 'Headman' and is bestowed on the candidate polling the greatest number of votes in the island elections, which are held every three years. An interesting requirements in the election of the eight councillors is that one of the successful candidates must be a woman.

Tristan da Cunha's isolated remoteness has resulted in intermarriage. Apart from two survivors from the brigantine "Italia" named Lavarello and Andrew Repetto, after their ship had foundered off the island in 1892, no new blood arrived to broaden the community's lineage until the late 1960s. Consequently among the three hundred Tristan da Cunhans there are only seven family names: Glass, Green, Hagan, Lavarello, Repetto, Rogers and Swain.

Because of its location Tristan da Cunha is destined to remain one of the loneliest and inaccessible outposts of civilisation in the world, but while in many ways life on the island remains unchanged from a century ago, the islanders today enjoy a standard of living comfort unimaginable before the development of their crayfish industry.

Because of her size, the RMS "St. Helena" is unable to berth alongside the jetty like the trawler "Atlantic Isle", but must needs lie at anchor off Hottentot Point. As the gale force winds which generally prevail limit the opportunity of discharging her anxiously awaiting cargo, four days are allocated to the mail-ship's call at Tristan da Cunha.

Weather permitting therefore, passengers have the unique opportunity of setting foot on an island, so divorced from Western civilisation that four young Tristan da Cunhans, carried in the mail-ship to Cape Town en route for England to train as carpenter, plumber, electrician and mechanic, had never before seen a two-storied building, let alone a car, a bus, or an aircraft.

Her annual pilgrimage to Tristan da Cunha accomplished the RMS "St. Helena" sets course for Cape Town, 1,500 miles almost due east of the island. After six days of comparative discomfort, despite stabilizers, caused by the traditional Cape Rollers, the mail-ship docks in Cape Town, where she prepares for the lengthy return passage, via the Islands, to her home port back in the United Kingdom.

VI THE SECOND RMS "St. HELENA"

As early as 1982 Curnow Shipping Limited realised the need to replace their mail-ship with a larger vessel, following a significant increase in demand for cargo space and accommodation between the United Kingdom and Cape Town.

Originally designed for service on the Vancouver to Alaska ferry run, the first RMS had maximum cargo capacity of 800 tons, and was not equipped to handle containerised freight. Furthermore, although the vessel could accommodate 76 passengers, once the Islanders had claimed their priority reservations, the demand for ocean travel by through passengers between the United Kingdom and the Cape far exceeded the remaining available berths. However as any replacement vessel would require a considerable outlay by the British Treasury, it is not surprising that four more years should elapse before the necessary funds were made available.

During 1986 the Foreign and Commonwealth Office announced its intention to provide a new cargo-passenger liner to replace the 23 year old "St.Helena" at an estimated cost of £19.5. million. The new ship would be the property of the St. Helenan Government, while the St. Helena Shipping Company was awarded a two year contract, from the time the new vessel came into service, to manage, operate and man her.

The design contract was awarded to Three Quays Marine Services in London, a member of the P & O Group, and with the knowledge and experience gained after 8 years in the Island trade, Curnow Shipping was able to contribute to a number of design features.

Twice the size of the first "St.Helena" the new ship was designed to lift 1,500 tons of cargo with a container capacity of 62 TEUs, some of which could be refrigerated. Available Government funds had limited her design cargo space, but provision was made in the vessel's design to permit her overall length to be stretched by 10 metres to provide additional freight capacity when the expense was justified.

Once the marine consultants had completed their design by August 1987, tenders were called for, Five shipbuilders responded, of which three, with shipyards in Aberdeen, Clydeside and Lowestoft, were short listed for consideration. Up to this point all was going well, and no one could foresee the astonishing saga of Government ineptitude, and political expediency, that was about to blight the construction of the first passenger ship to operate a liner service to be built in a British Shipyard since 1964.

The marine consultants had misgivings over Government plans to accept the lowest tender, submitted by Hall Russell Ltd. of Aberdeen, as the company was unable to furnish a financial guarantee adequate to cover the construction and post-delivery period. Financial consultants to

RMS ST HELENA II at Cape Town, 1992

(P. C. Kohler)

the Overseas Development Administration considered however that Hall Russell should just be able to survive with the contract to build the new mail-ship. They did nonetheless add a proviso that a possibility did exist that the shipyard might be compelled to shut down before the contract was completed.

Following receipt of the financial consultant's report, the marine consultant set out the situation as they assessed it. It read as follows:-

To survive, Hall Russell Ltd. would need to negotiate an additional order, or equivalent contract. Failing that, an injection of more capital. Or, as a last resort, if the first two alternatives could not be realised, an increase in the price to build the ship.

This should have the effect of narrowing the price difference between the tenders submitted by the other two shipyards short-listed, thereby negating the reason for risking the placing of the contract with Hall Russell Ltd. in the first place. In the light of the prevailing circumstances, the marine consultants then advised Her Majesty's Government to set down specific financial requirements which Hall Russell would have to fulfill, before being awarded the contract to build the new ship.

The Overseas Development Administration thereupon consulted with both the Department of Trade and Industry, and the Ministry of Defence, in the light of their expertise in negotiating shipping contracts, and guarantees. The Ministry of Defence expressed the opinion that the guarantee of £2.4 million offered by Hall Russell Ltd. to secure the contract represented only approximately 50% of what they would expect to receive. Upon receipt of the view expressed by the Ministry of Defence, the Overseas Development Administration decided against awarding the construction contract to Hall Russell Ltd. Instead they favoured the third lowest tender at an extra cost of £1.9 million, whose bid was technically superior to, and marginally higher than, the second lowest.

At this point in the negotiations the Industry Department for Scotland got into the act. In their view they were not convinced that the grounds for setting aside the Hall Russell's tender were adequate, and that the financial guarantees the Overseas Development Administration had required of Hall Russell were too stringent. The Industry Department contended that their assessment was based on the good reputation Hall Russell Ltd. enjoyed; the good track record of their new yard manager; and the fact that there were a number of potential orders which the company was actively pursuing, to which their yard's expertise was particularly suited.

In addition, the Industry Department for Scotland concluded that the net risk to public funds, in the event of Hall Russell Ltd. being placed in receivership, should not exceed £200,000 after taking into account the yard's guarantee of £2.4 million, and the £1.9 million between the tender price submitted by Hall Russell Ltd. and that of the third lowest, preferred by the Overseas Development Administration because of the financial risk involved.

Because, in their opinion, the financial risk was relatively small, the Industry Department for Scotland believed the Administration would be justified in placing the order with Hall Russell Ltd., as without it the yard would fail, with associated social and economic consequences. The Department also took into account the wider economic difficulties experienced in Scotland at the time, in the shipbuilding, steel, and off-shore oil and gas industries, these in the last instance particularly heavily on Aberdeen.

In a subsequent report by the Comptroller and Auditor-General published on June 29, 1990 it was revealed that the National Audit Office was unable to find documentary evidence to support the opinions expressed by the Industry Department for Scotland.

However, despite the Industry Department's representations the Administration repeated its preference to accept the third lowest tender at the increased cost of £1.9 million. The Scottish Office thereupon proposed transfer to the Overseas Development Administration of any amounts required to meet the cost of completing the proposed ship above the tender price, and allowing for Hall Russell's guarantee of £2.4 million, should the shipyard fail to honour the contract.

The Treasury approved this unusual arrangement, subject to the cost being forthcoming from the Overseas Development Administration's resources, and, if necessary, from the Scottish Office's existing Public Expenditure Survey provision. And on November 26, 1987 Ministers agreed that, subject to negotiation, the contract to build the new "St.Helena" should be awarded to Hall Russell Ltd. of Aberdeen, and construction on the vessel began.

However, from as early as February 1988 it became apparent that Hall Russell was experiencing difficulties in financing the undertaking, and by the end of October the marine consultants expressed concern as to the continued financial stability of the yard. Early in November Hall Russell Ltd. was placed in receivership by its Bankers, with debts of several million pounds owing to over 80 creditors.

At this moment of time construction of the "St. Helena" was one third complete, up to schedule, and technically satisfactory, while the Overseas Development Administration had disbursed to the yard £7.2 million in stage payments. To allow time to consider the options available, the Overseas Development Administration, acting on behalf of the Government of St. Helena, negotiated with the Receivers to continue financing the vessel's construction in receivership on a short term basis, at a labour cost of approximately £140,000 per week, plus the cost of essential materials. The work that was then executed, amounting to a further £4.1 million, was restricted to such as was necessary to allow the ship to be completed in another yard, should the necessity arise.

On December 23, 1988 the Overseas Development Administration asked the marine consultants to invite tenders for the completion of the ship, to which seven companies replied. Four of the seven incorporated in their tenders offers to the Receivers for the purchase of the shipyard, wishing to complete the vessel in situ. The other three companies proposed completion of the ship in their own shipyards.

After further consultation with the Industry Department for Scotland and with the Receivers, the Overseas Development Administration narrowed the choice to two shipbuilders. The two were Zenta Engineering Ltd with ship-repair yards on both the Clyde and the Tyne, and A.P.Appledore International Ltd a subsidiary of the A & P Appledore Group, with ship-repair yards at Falmouth, on the Tyne, and at other locations in the United Kingdom. Both companies had proposed the completion of the "St.Helena" at the Hall Russell shipyard in Aberdeen, which they were prepared to purchase from the Receivers.

The consultants favoured Appledore as a better financial risk than Zenta Engineering, and recommended their tender be accepted, although £1.5 million higher than the bid submitted by Zenta. But whereas Appledore offered a full warranty on the complete vessel, Zenta did not. However, the Industry Department for Scotland favoured Zenta's offer as promising a better long term prospect for shipbuilding and marine employment in Aberdeen.

Negotiations between the two companies and the overseas Development Administration continued into February 1989, when Zenta Engineering withdrew their favourable offer to purchase the Hall Russell shipyard from the Receivers for a consideration of £500,000 paid to them by Appledore, in the light of the work carried out on the ship during the receivership, to reduce their tender price to complete the "St.Helena" by £500,000. In addition, Appledore submitted a higher offer to the Receivers for the shipyard than had Zenta, conditional on them receiving an increase of £600,000 on their tendered price to complete the vessel.

After yet further consultations with the Industry Department for Scotland, and after seeking legal advice, the Overseas Development Administration considered that the safest way to protect the Government's position would be to accept the increase in the contract price, in the knowledge that the Receivers would have disposed of the Hall Russell shipyard to Appledore to best advantage. Consequently on February 20 the contract to complete the "St.Helena" was awarded to Appledore on their terms as finally amended during the protracted negotiations that had taken place.

The "St. Helena" was duly launched by His Royal Highness The Prince Andrew, Duke of York, on October 31, 1989, and sailed on her maiden voyage on November 14, 1990, eleven months later than originally planned and anticipated. The final cost of construction is estimated at £32.34 million, an increase of £12.8 million or 66 per cent on the original contract price of £19.5 million. The Scottish Office's liability, arising from it indemnifying the Overseas Development Administration at the time the original contract was awarded to Hall Russell was estimated at £11 million.

Costing a fraction over £4,773 per gross registered ton to build, the "St.Helena" must rate as the most costly convential cargo-passenger liner launched to date! The whole sorry story highlights the futility of allowing untoward political factors to influence the negotiation of a strictly business contract.

At the time the original decision was taken by the Overseas Development Administration, continued employment for 475 workers in the Hall Russell/Appledore Aberdeen shipyard was envisaged, as a tangible return for awarding the contract to Hall Russell in the first place. It is ironic therefore that in the April 1991 issue of "Ships Monthly" a brief news item contained the announcement that A & P Appledore, following the completion of passenger vessel "St.Helena" the previous year, had closed their Aberdeen shipyard.

Despite the misfortunes that beset her construction, resulting in an eleven month delay in the vessel coming into service, the new RMS "St.Helena" has more than lived up to expectations. A fine example of British craftmanship this cargo-passenger liner has been designed and constructed to the highest standards, while the decor and furnishing of her public rooms and staterooms is reminiscent of the Union-Castle liners that graced the Cape run for so many years. This is not surprising, as the decor was carried out by Ron Baxter who had been closely associated with the design and furnishing of those "Castle" liners constructed from 1959 onwards.

The 6,767 gross registered ton "St.Helena" measures 105 metres in length, has a beam of 19.5 metres, and when down to her marks draws 6 metres. Passenger accommodation is provided for 100 persons, plus 28 inter-island berths, while provision has also been made to accommodate 4 students attending the marine faculty at The Prince Andrew School in St. Helena. The entire passenger and crew accommodation is fully air-conditioned.

The mail-ship is manned by 18 officers, all of whom are British, and 38 petty officers and ratings. Apart from the officers, the remainder of the ship's company, including galley staff, stewards and stewardesses, are all native St. Helenans.

Although designed to lift 1,500 tons of cargo, the vessel has in fact the capacity to carry 1,600 tons, loaded through two hatches, both forward of the Bridge structure. The main hatch is on the foredeck with the second smaller hatch located on the fo'c'sle head. They are served by two Hagglunds cranes with a lifting capacity of 12.5 tons, which can operate in tandem to handle 25 tons in a single lift.

The "St.Helena" is built to handle and stow 62 twenty foot containers, as well as break-bulk cargo. There are two deep tanks for the transport of oil cargo, as well as facilities under the break of the fo'c'sle for carrying livestock, and provisions for the storage of motor vehicles.

The Vessel carries virtually everything essential to the needs of the Islanders other than petrol, which is prohibited cargo in ships registered to carry passengers. Between shipments out of Cardiff and Cape Town, some 9,000 tons of freight is carried to the islands annually, which in turn provide exports amounting to only 250 tons, mainly dried, canned and frozen fish.

The "St. Helena" boasts twin screws, each shaft driven by a Mirrlees Blackstone 6K Major diesel engine, although gas oil is burnt while man-oeuvering in harbour. Each shaft turns a 3,500 mm diameter high-skewed controllable-pitch propellor, while the vessel is fitted with a single semi-balanced rudder, and with Brown Bros. fin-type stabilizers. The ship's designed service speed is 14.5 knots, and at maximum revolutions 16 knots, although 18 knots was comfortably maintained when carrying out acceptance trials in the North Sea.

In outward appearance the "St.Helena" is a handsome ship, although to the purist her overall length, limited to 105 metres, gives the vessel a somewhat dumpy silhouette. This present short-coming will be overcome when circumstances permit the lengthening of her hull.

The new livery adopted by the St. Helena Shipping Company, of royal blue hull, white upperworks, cranes and masts; and a pale yellow funnel embossed with the emblem of the old East India Company, is a happy choice, and has been well accepted by the Islanders who chose the colour scheme themselves in 1988.

The distinctive elliptical funnel rises behind the signal mast mounted aft of the wheelhouse. The navigation Bridge is particularly spacious, and passengers are permitted access to this holy of holies when the vessel is at sea. Access is also allowed to the area above the wheelhouse deckhead, which provides an excellent viewing platform when leaving or entering harbour.

The Bridge is designed with an amidships navigation station abaft the control console, with a chart table fitted on the port wing of the Bridge, close to the forward bulkhead, for use in port approaches and other inshore areas.

The RMS "St.Helena" is equipped with every modern aid to navigation, including two Racal Decca Arpa radars; Racal Decca navigator; Navstar 602S radio navigator; Marconi depth sounder; remote draft and freeboard indicator; sea surface temperature recorder; controls for watertight doors throughout the ship; smoke detectors, and fire alarms.

The Bridge also houses a simplified data display of the engine monitoring systems. In addition to all engine and bearing pressures and temperatures, the computer monitors all the ship's vital signs, including it is reported, the temperatures of the ice-cream and the meat carried in the freezers!

The Radio Office is located just abaft the wheelhouse, and provides telephone kiosks for the convenience of passengers making radio-telephone calls while the vessel is on passage. Here again the Radio room is fitted with the most up-to-date equipment, the majority of which is supplied by STC International. It includes SS6 and VHF radios; radiotelegraphy; radio telex; satellite communication system; satellite navigator; weather facsimile; direction finder; and on-board telephone and broadcast systems.

The forward end of the Boat Deck is where the ship's officers have their accommodation. This includes comfortable bedrooms and dayrooms for the Master, the Chief Engineer, the Chief Officer, and the Second Engineer. And there are additional cabins for the lower ranking officers, cadets, and the four students from the marine facility at the Prince Andrew School at Jamestown.

Four lifeboats are carried, two mounted on either side of the Boat Deck, providing a degree of shade for passengers relaxing in steamer-chairs on the Promenade Deck below. Very rarely are the lifeboats employed as tenders, as at St. Helena passengers are ferried ashore in the Ship's Agents' longboats and at Ascension in the island's own motor launch.

The Promenade Deck houses Pursers' and additional cabins forward, and two of the vessel's four public rooms. There is a small intimate Quiet Lounge on the starboard side, shared by both passengers and officers, and in which is incorporated a very adequate library. Aft of the Quiet Lounge is the Children's Playroom, while on the port side opposite is a four-berth cabin with en suite facilities.

Finally, at the aft end of the Promenade Deck the Sun Lounge, with portside bar, opens onto the games deck, the one deck area covered in Malaysian teak. The outdoor tiled swimming pool is tucked in close to the windows of the Sun Lounge, and is protected from the wind by means of two longitudinal bulkheads that angle out to the ship's railings. And aft of the swimming pool, set flush with the teak decking, is the hatch allowing access for passengers' baggage, ship's stores, and the mail-room.

The main lounge is located forward, one deck down on 'A' Deck, stretching the full width of the ship and with clear views ahead and to both sides. A Bar is located on the portside, and a room divider permits a separate seating area, away from the bar, on the starboard side. Tasteful decor in soft pastel shades enhances the main Lounge, and similar motifs are carried through in the other three public rooms. The Lounge is directly accessible by a passenger lift from 'B' and 'C' Decks, in addition to a generously spacious stairwell.

In addition to the main Lounge, 'A' Deck houses the bulk of the standard outside staterooms, all with good sized window, and with private facilities comprising toilet, shower and wash-basin. There are fold-away upper and lower double cabins, as well as twin three and four-berth rooms. In most cabins there are individual wardrobes for each berth; a chest of drawers and a dressing-table with chair. The only shortcoming in the cabin furnishing, in the opinion of the author, is inadequate drawer space for a long ocean voyage, a minor inconvenience that could be easily rectified.

At the aft end of 'A' Deck is a well-equipped Launderette for the use of passengers; the Doctor's Surgery and the ship's Hospital, which has both a male and female ward. And it is of interest to note that one stateroom, located near the Hospital, is specially designed to accommodate physically handicapped travellers.

On the starboard side of 'B' Deck, one deck down, are eight additional passenger staterooms, all with portholes and like those on 'A' Deck with private facilities and similarly furnished while for those passengers preferring a tub to a shower, a bathroom is located at the aft end of the row of staterooms. Spacious and well-equipped crew accommodation runs the full length down the port side of 'B' Deck, as well as aft of the eight passenger staterooms on the starboard side, while the ship's Laundry is located in the stern of the vessel aft of the crew's quarters.

At the forward end of 'B' Deck, the Purser's Office, the Bureau, and a roomy walk-in, well-stocked Shop surround the main Entrance Foyer. The Foyer holds a special interest for ship-lovers, housing as it does a splendid display of beautifully crafted scale model ships, the creation of Radio Officer Bob Wilson, who has been honoured for his painstaking work by his elections as a Fellow of the Royal Society.

'C' Deck is the lowest passenger deck, where 28 berths, in small two and four berth cabins are located, designed as through-passage budget accommodation, as well as for the 48 inter-island shuttle between St.Helena and Ascension. Three of these cabins have private facilities, the remainder only a wash-basin, the occupants sharing communal showers and segregated toilets.

All through passengers must disembark at Jamestown while the mail-ship discharges cargo, makes the shuttle run to Ascension, and returns to St. Helena to load what freight is on offer. The 28 berths on 'C' Deck are employed to house the working party travelling to Ascension to commence their twelve month contracts, and to bring home those whose contracts have expired.

The Dining Saloon, which can seat up to 75 persons at each of two sittings, is located at the forward end of 'C' Deck on the starboard side, with tables accommodating from two to eight passengers and officers. The very spacious Galley, manned by a staff of five, occupies the port side of 'C' Deck. opposite to and adjoining the Dining Saloon. Fitted with the most up-to-date culinary equipment, the Galley's bulkheads and deckhead are clad in stainless steel in the interests of hygiene and cleanliness.

The crew Mess, and their 'Pig and Whistle', are situated aft of the Galley on the port side of 'C' Deck. Further aft are the specialised storerooms. Those cold-rooms in which meat, fish, dairy products, fruit and vegetables, ice-cream, and certain wines are stocked, are refrigerated at varying temperatures, all monitored from the Bridge. Additional storage for dry stores, beers and spirits, and cleaning materials are also located in this part of the vessel.

Below on 'D' Deck are the mail and baggage rooms, as well as essential services, workshops, the air-conditioning plant, the stabilizers, and everything connected with the Engineroom.

Overall the new RMS "St.Helena" compares very favourably with the liners of yester-year on the Cape run. She may be smaller and more compact than were the "Castle" giants, but more than holds her own when it comes to comfort, public amenities, and decor. Manned by the same officers and St. Helenans who created such a warm and friendly atmosphere on board her predecessor the first RMS, it is certain that this new mini-liner will also earn the reputation of being a 'Happy' ship.

The RMS "St.Helena" sailed from Cardiff Docks in South Wales on her maiden voyage to Table Bay on Monday November 14, 1990, and realised the expectations of her 'owner' Andrew Bell who, accompanied by his wife Prue, took passage to Cape Town.

"Not only did we find that she took more than her 1,500 tons of cargo" he said in an interview with the 'Cape Argus' following the vessel's arrival at the Cape 24 days later on December 8, "but she was also, as a result of her twin propellors, almost vibrationless!"

While her first southbound voyage to Cape Town was such a pronounced success, with the mail-ship comfortably maintaining a service speed of 16 knots, almost a knot and a half faster than anticipated; on her return journey homeward bound the RMS met up with serious trouble.

One of the inevitable teething troubles that had developed southbound for Table Bay was a cooling problem in the ship's port engine, but nothing serious enough to delay her scheduled arrival at the Cape. But after sailing from Tenerife on the final leg of her voyage home to Cardiff, the starboard engine developed similar cooling problems.

At 03.00 on the morning of January 5, 1991 a connecting rod in the starboard engine fractured, causing the vessel, as a precautionary measure, to limp into Lisbon on the port engine only at 40 percent power, to land her passengers. She docked in Lisbon at 19.00 that same evening, and her 63 passengers were flown to England to Gatwick airport, before the "St.Helena" slowly made her way up the Portuguese coastline to the port of Vigo in northern Spain to await instructions, before heading for Falmouth for repairs.

To Andrew Bell and his colleagues at Curnow Shipping this major set-back was a bitter disappointment. It was the first major breakdown the Line had suffered in 14 years, and to have occurred on their new vessel's maiden voyage was completely unexpected. Her predecessor, the first RMS had already been delivered to her new owners and was in Durban undergoing a major refit. So a replacement vessel had to be found, to take the "St. Helena's" place in the scheduled service to the Islands and the Cape, while major repairs were carried out on the new mail-ship.

To fill the gap the St. Helenan Government chartered the "Lowland Lancer", formerly the troopship RFA "Sir Lancelot", which had played a major role in the Falklands War in 1982 in the company of her sister-ships the RFAs "Sir Galahad" and "Sir Tristram". The RFA "Sir Lancelot" had been fortunate in surviving the conflict, for her two sisters were sunk by the enemy.

Built for the Ministry of Defence in 1963, "Sir Lancelot" was disposed of to the Lowline Company in 1989 and was operating in the Mediterranean. Fitted with bow and stern ramps for handling vehicles, as a troopship "Sir Lancelot" had accommodation for 340 troops, rising to 540 men under active service conditions, and her Sulzer diesel engines were designed to drive the vessel at 17 knots.

In her new role the "Lowland Lancer" was certified to carry 200 passengers, some in cabins, the remaineder in dormitories. She was therefore a far from ideal replacement for the RMS "St Helena", but she was the only ship readily available at the time. While the officers of the St. Helena Shipping Company in Porthleven and in Cape Town co-ordinated passenger bookings on behalf of Lowline passengers carried in the "Lowland Lancer" were on its owner's terms and conditions, not those of the St. Helena Line nor was the St. Helena Shipping Company in any way responsible for the onboard services, all of which were provided by the ship's owners.

It was perhaps unfortunate that wear and tear had left their mark on the "Lowland Lancer", insofar as her engines were concerned after 27 years in service. There were a series of mechanical problems experienced while the ship was on charter to the St. Helenan Government, which precluded the vessel from adhering to its scheduled time-table. Nonetheless the "Lowland Lancer" did complete two round voyages while the RMS "St. Helena" was effecting repairs in Falmouth, and the Government's commitment to the Islanders was honoured.

Repairs to the mail-ship in Falmouth necessitated the complete replacement of the starboard engine, and this was effected by cutting a rectangular hole in the ship's side and removing the damaged engine laterally. By March 25, 1991 a new starboard engine had been installed and the hull plating replaced. Sea trials commenced the following day and proved successful, allowing the RMS to sail from Falmouth to Cardiff Docks in South Wales on April 2, to prepare for her delayed Voyage 2 to the Islands and Table Bay.

The RMS "St. Helena" returned to her scheduled service on April 12, when she headed south on the second of what will be her scheduled sailings well into the 21st Century, and happily, for all concerned the round voyage was completed without incident. Voyage 3 too passed without anything untoward happening, but on Voyage 4 the RMS was once again headline news, on this occasion in a dramatic sea rescue operation.

On Friday afternoon, August 30. 1991, the RMS "St. Helena" anchored off Jamestown after completing the ferry run from Ascension. Bad weather and strong head winds had delayed her arrival in the sheltered bay by six hours, and was obviously the cause of the maritime disaster that was to occur within the relatively close proximity of the island.

As the RMS approached St. Helena, Radio Officer Bob Wilson had been asked whether the ship had been in radio contact with the "Oman

Sea One", a small 290 gross registered ton factory trawler, which had recently commenced crab fishing around the island and its neighbouring sea-mounts. No contact had been made.

The following day the RMS discharged the balance of her southbound cargo into lighters, and was about to load what freight was forthcoming from Cape Town, before sailing for Table Bay that evening. At that moment news began to filter in that the 130,257 deadweight Panamanian tanker "Ruth M" had chanced upon the sinking "Oman Sea One" at a position 90 nautical miles north-west of St. Helena. Only the fore part of the trawler was visible, ran the report, and the "Ruth M" had been able to rescue twelve survivors of the seventeen man crew from two inflatable life rafts. Those rescued included all the 'Saints' crewing in the trawler, and the British chief officer.

With a major maritime incident within his area of responsibility, the Governor of St. Helena, Mr. Alan Hoole, assumed control as rescue co-ordinate in a search for the missing crew members with immediate effect. A United States Air Force P3 Orion was summoned from Ascension to carry out an extensive aerial search of the area from an altitude of 500 feet, and while the "Ruth M" headed for Jamestown with her twelve survivors, a second vessel continued the search from the five missing men. This was the 24,080 deadweight "Padrone", Cyprus owned but on charter to Safmarine-Bank Lines, and employed on their North American-South African Service. In addition, the Fishery Protection vessel HMS "Dumbarton Castle", southbound to the Falklands, was diverted to the scene of the wreck.

With immediate despatch the RMS "St. Helena" sailed for the disaster area in a south-easterly gale registering Force 8 on the Beaufort scale. Assisted by a following sea the RMS steamed on her errand of mercy at maximum revolutions, logged at 18 knots, reaching the stricken trawler by 22.00 that evening. With the invaluable aid of his ship's searchlights, Captain Bob Wyatt located the bow of the "Oman Sea One", all that remained above the surface, and in the company of the "Padrone" began a systematic search of the area. Fortunately during the night the weather moderated, which was to assist in rescue operations, but by dawn a heavy sea and swell were still present.

As dawn broke at 06.00 GMT on Sunday September 1, the bow of the sinking trawler was seen for the last time as it sank beneath the waves, while simultaneously a life-jacketed survivor was sighted in the immediate vicinity. Captain Wyatt thereupon lowered his No. 2 lifeboat with Chief Officer Bob Hone in charge, and the trawler's cook Rafael Demedia was picked up at 07.30.

Demedia had wisely remained in the fo'c'sle of the "Oman Sea One" for the 48 hours that elapsed following the sudden capsize of his ship, and heartened by the sight of the "St. Helena's" searchlights had had the presence of mind to remain where he was until daylight. In the heavy seas still prevailing the recovery of the lifeboat was a far from easy manoeuvre, but good seamanship ensured a safe return alongside the RMS where it was hoisted back on board.

In the course of that Sunday the P3 Orion sighted a third life raft, and directed the "Padrone" to its location, but sadly it was found to be unoccupied. A good deal of wreckage was sighted in the area of search, but there was no sign of the missing men—the British Master, two engineers, and a second cook.

With the sea temperature registering 20 Celsius, and advised that at that temperature persons could survive in the water for up to four days, Governor Alan Hoole requested the RMS "St. Helena" to continue her search for the missing seamen until 17.00 hrs on Monday September 2, before returning to Jamestown. The extended search for further survivors proved fruitless, and abandoning the area the RMS returned to Jamestown. arriving back in the anchorage that same night.

Loading was completed by the evening of Tuesday September, 3, and the mail-ship sailed for Cape Town, four days behind schedule, with seven of the "Oman Sea One's" survivors on board, and with the satisfaction of contributing to the safe recovery of all but four of the seventeen man crew.

It was not the first time that a British built liner had suffered an early setback in recent years. The Cunard "Queen Elizabeth 2" ten times the size of the RMS, experienced a major engineering problem when she first came into service. And on her maiden voyage to Australia, P & O's, liner "Canberra" was compelled to stop over at Malta to effect generator repairs.

It is surprising that in negotiating a new contract with the St. Helena Shipping Company to manage, operate and man the new RMS "St. Helena", the Overseas Development Administration, on behalf of the Government of St. Helena, stipulated only a two year period, calculated from the date the new mail-ship came into service. The initial contract, signed in 1977 was for ten years, subsequently extended for a further three years pending the arrival of the new ship. For a company to have carried out such an efficient operation to the satisfaction of all concerned for a period of 13 years is no small achievement.

However, on September 23, 1992 the Overseas Development Administration announced that the St. Helena Shipping Company had been awarded a further three year contract to come into effect in November. it is to be hoped therefore that Curnow Shipping Limited, through the medium of the St. Helena Shipping Company, will continue to control the destiny of the new RMS "St. Helena" for many years to come. It took Andrew Bell much courage to enter a trade forsaken by shipping companies of international stature and to succeed against the weight of professional opinion is a remarkable accomplishment. The first RMS "St. Helena" established herself, against all the odds, as a welcome replacement for the Union Castle liners that had provided a scheduled mail, passenger and freight service to the Islands and the Cape for more than a century. The second RMS "St. Helena" has the added advantage of increased cargo capacity, more passenger accommodation, and improved public facilities for the ocean traveller, to build on the reputation so firmly established by her predecessor.

Long may the "Saints" sail on!

RMS ST HELENA I (Curnow Shipping)

(Curnow)

BIBLIOGRAPHY

Publications:

Controller and Auditor General, British Government — Report dated June 29, 1990

Brown, Eric — "Cardiff Docks" — Published by King Alfred Books Ltd.

Cross, Tony — "St. Helena" — Published by David Charles

Hughes, D and Humphries, P. — "In South African Waters" — Published by Oxford University Press

Ingham, Brian and Pabst, Robert — "Maritime South Africa" — Published by C. Struik

Kohler, Peter — "Tradition Finds a Place in St. Helena's Ocean Lifeline" — Published in the magazine "Sea Breezes"

Lofthouse, Marjorie — "The New Adventurers" — Published by Enterprise B.B.C.

McCall, Bernard — "Barry Docks in the 1980s" — Published by Bernard McCall

Mitchell, W.H. and Sawyer, L.A. — "The Cape Run" — Published by Terence Dalton Ltd.

Myhill, Henry — "The Canary Islands" — Published by Faber & Faber Ltd.

"Ships Monthly" Magazine

"South African Shipping News and Fishing Industry Review" Magazine

"Sunday Telegraph" March 1978

Teale, P.L. — "The Island of St. Helena" — Published by the Royal Institution of Chartered Surveyors

Winchester, Simon — "Outpost" — Published by Hodder and Stoughton.

Young, Gavin — "Slow Boats Home" — Published by Hutchinson

INDEX

150

"Windsor Castle" (III):	53.55.75	Wolff, Gustav:	16
Woermann, Adolph:	16	"World Rennaissance":	68
Woermann Line:	21.25.35.40	Wyatt, Capt. Robert:	73.144